Subplots to a C

Ten Years of In Certain Places

Edited by
Charles Quick, Elaine Speight,
and Gerrie van Noord

Published by
In Certain Places, Preston

Table of Contents

Foreword
John Newling

In September 1971, as a hesitant and anxious teenager, I went to Burslem, a town in the potteries, to study art. I carried with me a drizzle of contradictions, uncertainties and doubts about art and about myself.

One of the first things I made as a student was a working table football machine, destined for the local pub where I met my friends. It broke. Later I dug holes along a canal towpath, spending many hours chatting with passers-by about art and stuff; at times it was the stuff that seemed more interesting. Most days saw me carrying lithography plates into cafes, pubs and parks to collect drawings and texts made by people I met; most nights I would print that day's layer.

I was never wholly sure of what I was doing, but I know I was asking many questions of myself and of art. These flurries of questions seemed to be generated in certain places that felt like laboratories of art, for me to play and learn in. Place, materially and metaphorically, became a very real constituent of my work. For me every place held within it a temporary threshold, the crossing of which opened a space in which to move, think, explore, exchange and express ideas. These were spaces that could meld with our common views of place, while allowing a shift in our agreed sense of it.

Thirty-four years later, in 2005, I was invited to develop a project

for In Certain Places. This was a partnership that had begun two years earlier, in 2003, between the Harris Museum & Art Gallery in Preston and the University of Central Lancashire. Led by Professor Charles Quick, who was in 2005 joined by Elaine Speight, the aim was to produce a programme of temporary public artworks, residencies and events to involve artists in the development of a city.

Much older, but still asking questions and exploring places, I made my first visit to the city of Preston upon Elaine and Charles's invitation. The journey took me across the Pennines and north into Lancashire. My first impression was that the city was neat, walkable and a good place to wander and think. It had the geographical markers that open a city up to art; a river, (abandoned) industrial sites, a grand market place, a cavernous bus station, a museum and library, shops, parks, wealthy areas, poor areas, all of them thresholds to exchanges and the contextual disorientations that art can bring.

I met Charles and Elaine at the Harris Museum. I learnt that the museum had been a civic aspiration that began with public fundraising in the 1850s, before being made a reality by the bequest of Robert Harris, a Preston lawyer, in 1877. I was already aware of Preston as active in its political structure and of its civic aspirations. This condition, one of possibilities built through experience within a tradition of civic ambition, is a fine ground for a project like In

Certain Places to flourish. After that first visit, I left Preston knowing that it was a place where I could develop a work. I was enthused by the market place, both architecturally and as a site of exchange. I also sensed that Speight and Quick were a strong, knowledgeable and serious team, looking for new strategies for art in a city that would be open to innovation.

Preston has a long history of civic involvement. Built on a foundation of trade and craft guilds, the city has a tradition of allegiance, aligned to the welfare of its citizens. Public declarations of guild loyalty to the mayor and to the city have been part of its structure, which has meant the city has had to regularly review its values. In Certain Places makes Speight and Quick part of this tradition. In Certain Places is in itself also a craft and a trade that seeks innovative possibilities for art and examines the effects that art has on the city; it is a guild of a kind.

The Preston Market Mystery Project was the project I proposed. It involved three separate installations in the market place. The events were connected and followed each other sequentially. They involved a working market stall, a live reading at dusk, and a meal, cooked on site. Each phase was complex in its organisation and required a great deal of logistical and technical support, and was incredibly well served by Quick, Speight and Kerenza McClarnan, who was co-opted into the project. I was struck by how exceptionally well linked the team was to resources within Preston. This local network meant they could respond quickly and were an exciting team to work with.

In Certain Places does not advocate art as an elixir of urban regeneration.

Rather the art is allowed to inhabit a city in a manner that slips off the edges of many subjects. The works accumulate to a point where their mass becomes infectious, and the city catches on to the excitement. An ecosystem like this is hard work, but, in the end, it embeds itself alongside the already existing histories and becomes part of a city's soil.

The relationship between project managers, curators and local politics is crucial. In successive visits I saw how Speight and Quick were building strong communications between themselves and the city council. City councils have a lot to do and often the art that comes to their city is very low on their radar. In order to be seen and supported, art groups need to convince them that they and their work have a place in their city, and that risk can be a positive experience. Speight and Quick have done this through discussions on re-configuring the city and the possibilities in seeing it as a living organism needing distinct resources to thrive. Their skills and knowledge have proved remarkably successful in bringing the city council to the table.

The presence of a university in the city is important. Students bring more than money to the area; they bring a willingness to enjoy art in all its experimental manifestations. They add to the critical mass so essential for art to thrive. Here there is another thread to the strategy of In Certain Places; the postgraduate course, run at the University of Central Lancashire by Professor Charles Quick and Professor Lubaina Himid, involves site and archive interventions. This programme of study is an exceptional grounding for artists who review place

and its histories, and who make work
in and through communities. It has
become a course that is imbued with
the ethos of In Certain Places.

All this creates a beautifully coherent
framework that has evolved over time,
generating challenging art at all levels.
Even a cursory glance at In Certain
Places' website shows the scale of
the projects that have populated the
programme, and pays testament to
the excellence of the artists they have
worked with.

In Certain Places is a maturing force.
It has joined a rich history of groups
and agencies in the UK and abroad
that have made significant contributions
to a broader understanding of
what art is and can be. The projects
are successful and add up to a
rapidly moving series of innovations
and experiments that keep art fluid
and vital. These experiments do
affect all our cities and towns, and,
most importantly, the people who live
in them.

CITIES

BETWEEN

Subplots, Tactics and Stories-so-Far
Elaine Speight

There is, currently, only one visible sign of In Certain Places' activities in Preston city centre. This can be found between platforms three and four of the railway station, on the windows of its waiting room. Amid discarded newspapers and the smell of disinfectant, travellers check their smartphones and train times and read magazines beneath the high-vaulted Victorian ceiling. Around them, shimmering snippets of text tell a fragmented story of travel, of waiting... dreaming... running... between cities... to distant peninsulas beyond. Installed in 2012, this work by the artist Lisa Wigham changes and shifts with the light. During the day it catches the sun before dissolving into the shadows, while at night, backlit by florescent lights, the words send glowing messages to passengers on trains that roll slowly through the darkened station to cities and towns further along the line.[1]

It seems fitting that this shifting artwork, with its themes of transit and flow, should constitute the only physical traces of our work. In Certain Places has always been an inherently liminal project, which variously appears and disappears from view, and is difficult to pin down. An ongoing series of conversations, relationships, events and artworks, it exists at the thresholds between university and city, art and urban development, public and private, inside and out. Initiated in 2003, by Charles Quick – then Senior Lecturer in Public Art at the University of Central Lancashire – and James

Green – former Programmes Manager at the Harris Museum & Art Gallery – In Certain Places began life as a partnership between UCLan and Preston City Council. In-between institutions and lacking a base, the project grew up in the city's public spaces. Until 2013 – when, to simplify life, we took up exclusive residence at UCLan – curatorial conversations, project planning and meetings with artists and funders generally took place in Preston's cafes, parks and squares. Allowing us to sample the menus of every eating-place in town, this ad-hoc, nomadic experience rubbed off on our practice. Combined with our close involvement with the city and its two main institutions, this fluidity of movement shaped our curatorial approach, and made In Certain Places the interesting, yet enigmatic, project it has become.

In the early 2000s, when In Certain Places emerged, attempts were underway to create a new identity for Preston, as they were in many post-industrial cities. While the Tithebarn regeneration scheme promised to transform it into a gleaming 'retail hub', branding exercises, such as the much-derided 'Third City' ambition – which sought to position Preston as the third city of the North West, after Manchester and Liverpool – attempted to shake off the city's mill town image and reinvent it as a significant urban centre. During this era of 'urban renaissance', conversations about art and culture were characterised by notions of the iconic. Monumental artworks, such as the *Angel of the North* (1998), were celebrated as a way to transform post-industrial places into cultural destinations, and cities sought to instigate their own 'Bilbao effect' by constructing shiny starchitect-designed museums and art galleries.[2] Yet, despite an early and aborted foray into large-scale regeneration, during which Charles Quick and Alfredo Jaar were appointed as lead artists in the Tithebarn master-planning stage, In Certain Places has always been more concerned with the existing realities of a place than with high-profile urban spectacles or imaginary futures.

Our interest in understanding, rather than re-branding, the city stems partly from the knowledge that ostensibly transformative projects, such as the *Angel of the North*, are often the culmination of a sustained cultural engagement with a place. However, the grounded nature of In Certain Places also derives from its origins as a conversation between an artist and a curator, who had each spent over a decade working, thinking, eating, shopping, talking, walking and dreaming in Preston. When I joined the team in 2005, fresh from university, I arrived with my own narratives of the place. Growing up on its rural fringe, I regularly travelled into the city, and its nightclubs, shopping centres and hidden places provide backdrops for memories of my teenage years. In the conversation with Lubaina Himid, printed in this book, the artist, a long-time critical friend of the project, questions the relationship between In Certain Places and Preston. Specifically, she wonders whether the city is simply somewhere we happen to be, or if it is the perfect location for our curatorial approach. Having

reflected on this question, I think that the answer is probably both. As a small, walkable city, with a university, an art gallery, a wealth of historic buildings, and beautiful, vast public spaces, Preston provides the ideal environment for a project about place. Yet, more than a curatorial context, it has also shaped our lives. Personally and professionally, the city is part of our provenance.

In his essay, Jonathan Vickery observes that for In Certain Places the city is 'not simply a backdrop, plinth or urban "stage", but often the subject, content and medium of art.' To this, I would add that it is also a collaborative partner. The artworks that we have commissioned embody the thoughts, ideas, experiences, desires, frustrations and knowledge of artists, yet they are made possible through the talents and practices of hundreds of other people. Over the last decade, we have worked with retail managers, actors, youth workers, students, cafe owners, electricians, market traders, vicars, health and safety officers, computer experts, urban designers, hairdressers, fashion trend analysts, museum attendants, park officers, transport managers, musicians, brewers and dancers, among others, to realise our projects. Rather than simply audience or participants, these people play important roles in the development of the work, and are interlocutors in our continuing conversations with the city.

Unlike many of the art and regeneration projects that surfaced in the early 2000s, In Certain Places has never aligned itself with the social cohesion agendas that became particularly prevalent in the UK under New Labour. Instead, our projects are created *with* rather than *for* different people in Preston. Originally titled

'Here + Now', the temporary public art strand was designed to initiate discussions about what public art could be, and to explore the effect artists could have upon the form and feel of a place. The accompanying programme of talks and debates – initially called 'Speaking of Art' – provided a forum for these conversations. By presenting examples of successful art and architectural projects in other UK cities, alongside the research of economists, sociologists, historians and geographers, the programme provoked new understandings and ideas about place, and generated a sense of excitement surrounding Preston's creative potential.

These activities contributed to a critical mass of people, who were keen to develop their own creative practices in, and through, the city. In addition to the pub discussions that followed each talk and debate, other conversations about artistic practice and place began to emerge in Preston in the mid-2000s. Facilitated by initiatives such as the 'Site and Place' and 'Archive Intervention' pathways of the Fine Art MA at UCLan (which later merged to become 'Site and Archive'), the opening of PAD – a Council-run gallery set up to support Lancashire artists – and Plaited Fog – an artists' discussion group, which I initiated in 2005, so called because of the perceived impossibility of bringing Preston artists together – these conversations provided the starting points for new creative ventures. One of these was Prestival, a three-day multi-sited event that artists Rebecca Chesney, Robina Deakin and I collectively devised in 2007. Appropriating In Certain Places' connections and approach, Prestival infiltrated the city's public spaces with the work of artists from Germany and the UK, including Preston. With limited funds, the project was driven by the energy and enthusiasm of the 40 artists involved, and contributed to a growing sense of vitality in the city.

Unfortunately, as in many places, the credit crunch of 2008 and subsequent recession replaced this sense of excitement with a growing lethargy. For some people, the drawn-out decline of the Tithebarn scheme, which was eventually officially abandoned in 2011, marked the end of the city's ambitions, while national budget cuts and the withdrawal of funds for initiatives such as PAD, indicated dwindling support for the arts.[3] Despite this, however, our conversations with the city have continued, and, alongside the activities of other creative people, produced shifts in its fabric and thinking. While the influence of our individual artworks and events may often be imperceptible, collectively they have helped to shape particular urban approaches. In this book, Preston City Council's Principal Urban Designer, Nigel Roberts, describes how In Certain Places encouraged him and his colleagues to generate their own creative solutions to some of the city's problems, rather than simply waiting for a commercial developer to take control. Similarly, Charles Quick's text 'Amplifying Civic Space' traces the incremental effects of our activities upon the city's Market Square. Unlike the top-down, all-encompassing approach of the Tithebarn scheme, this ongoing dialogue has inspired a more intuitive, intimate and slow-burning engagement.

In his essay, Paul O'Neill outlines a model of curating as 'an always-emergent praxis', through which a 'constellation of activities' develops over time. As a 'continuous space of negotiation' within a specific location, In Certain Places is an inherently, and necessarily, open-ended process. However, the durational nature of our work was never predetermined. Scheduled to take place between 2004 and 2008, the temporary public artworks and the programme of talks and debates were initially designed to inform and support the Tithebarn Lead Artist scheme, yet they ultimately outlived it. Like Lisa Wigham's installation, which, conceived as a temporary intervention, remains in the waiting room because nobody has asked for it to be taken down, In Certain Places persists, in part, because there is no desire for it to end. By allowing us the time to build relationships and to gain trust within the city, this long-term way of working has become central to our approach. As John Newling evocatively puts it in his foreword, it has taken time for us to develop our particular 'ecosystem' in Preston and to become part of the city's 'soil'.

Our open-ended curatorial approach could also be seen as part of what Michel de Certeau describes as a tactical engagement with a place. According to de Certeau, 'A *tactic* is a calculated action determined by the absence of a proper locus', which facilitates 'an art of being in between'.[4] Lacking the facilities and resources of larger organisations, we have survived by being fleet of foot, and grasping opportunities at the very moment they appear. Aside from the valuable support of Philippa Roddam, who, between 2008 and 2011, worked part-time as our project assistant, the last six years of In Certain Places have been delivered through the combined capacity of four working days per week. Similarly, our funding, although generous at times, has only ever been

secured for a three-year period at the most. Nevertheless, it is partly thanks to its precarious nature that In Certain Places endures. Our limited resources have forced us to be social and inventive, to exploit our connections to the city's institutions, and join forces with other people. One of our most recent ventures, *Harris Flights*, for instance, was realised with the help of Preston City Council and other local groups, while Shezad Dawood's *Piercing Brightness* was supported by national organisations, including Modern Art Oxford and Newlyn Art Gallery and The Exchange.

This tactical and fluid way of working, however, is not without its drawbacks, and can sometimes be a cause of confusion and distress. Where possible, we extend our open-ended methods to the artists we commission. We avoid fixed deadlines and projected outcomes in favour of ongoing dialogue and a commitment to help realise whatever the artist wishes to produce. Indeed, the only stipulation for most of our commissions is that they respond to the social and physical specificities of Preston and are developed in the city. While not unique, this remains a relatively unusual approach, and for many artists, particularly those at earlier stages in their careers, such flexible boundaries can prove daunting. Lisa Wigham, for example, talks about the struggle to locate a context for her work, while Katja van Driel describes the challenges posed by the lack of physical and institutional infrastructure within In Certain Places. In addition, the itinerant nature of our practice makes it hard to pin us down, and knowing how, when and where to approach us has proved a challenge for some. The non-art environment in which we work can also raise issues.

Subplots, Tactics and Stories-so-Far

By operating in a city one is subject to its – sometimes unwritten – rules, and the production of even a small and seemingly straightforward artwork can require months of negotiation. This is accompanied by a lack of control, which some artists can find frustrating. What might, at one moment, appear to be a definite plan can suddenly unravel, as the wants and needs of the city trump the requirements of the art. Once realised, the artworks must also fight for visibility and struggle to hold their own among the cacophony of urban life. Removed from the cultural context of a gallery, audiences can find it difficult to know how to respond, particularly when they do not realise that what they are experiencing is art. Yet, at the same time, this 'rubbing up' against everyday life is what gives good art its strength. In her text, Becky Shaw talks about the power of the 'frameless encounter'. Drawing on the concept of the 'meniscus', developed by Allan Kaprow to discuss the social edges of art, she describes the production of public artwork as a mutual dialogue with a place. She suggests that, when ostensibly well conceived and robust ideas fail, it is not because they are wrong, but because something significant is being revealed about the place and its relationship to the work.

When spoken aloud, the name 'In Certain Places' is often misheard and mistaken for similar misnomers. My favourites among these are 'Uncertain Places' and 'Insert In Places' as they touch on aspects of our work. In reality, however, we lifted the title from a passage in the novel *Invisible Cities* by Italo Calvino. In the book, the merchant and traveller Marco Polo regales the Mongolian emperor with tales of what appear to be disparate cities in foreign lands, but in fact are all versions of the narrator's native Venice. Recounting tales of 'thin cities', 'hidden cities', 'trading cities', 'continuous cities', full of 'eyes', 'names' and 'signs', Polo conjures somewhere that is, at once, familiar and unknown. In the same way, the artworks and conversations that make up In Certain Places tell a fragmented, tangential story of Preston as a creative, frustrating, secretive, surprising and continually evolving place. In her essay Sophie Hope describes the project as 'navigating a critical path' through a series of 'stories-so-far', which create 'comforting, disturbing and constantly unfolding scenarios on the city's stage'. This publication constitutes another section of that path. Arranged thematically, to provoke new readings of the work, it positions the voices of our collaborators alongside wider cultural debates. A comma, rather than a full stop, it signals a pause within the flow. It is a chance for us to catch our breath, look back at what we have learnt, and gather our resources before beginning the next chapter of a story, which began in certain places.

1. The title *Subplots to a City* was taken from a novel by Lisa Wigham.

2. The 'Bilbao effect' refers to the perceived change in the city's fortunes, following its regeneration and the opening of the Frank Gehry designed Guggenheim Museum in 1997.

3. To save money, PAD was closed in 2010, four years after it had opened.

4. Michel de Certeau, *The Practice of Everyday Life*, University of California Press, 1984, p.37 and p.30.

Histories of Regeneration
Charles Quick

I first travelled to Preston by British Rail in 1980, having been sent on a mission to take a photograph for a publisher. Then, seeking out the bus station, I travelled to Longridge. Once there I sought out Club Row, reported to be the world's oldest surviving housing financed through a building society, consisting of an unimposing terrace of twenty cottages, which was erected between 1794 and 1804.[1]

Ten years later I visited Preston again. This time to begin work as a lecturer in Sculpture and Public Art at Lancashire Polytechnic, two years before the next Guild celebrations were due. The first engagement with the city as an artist and educator was when my colleague Val Murray and I proposed and organised a temporary city-centre sculpture trail of site-specific artwork created by second-year Sculpture students on the BA course as part of the 1992 Preston Guild. By this time Lancashire Polytechnic had become a university, like many others had. In December 1993, students collaborated with inmates at Garth Prison to produce a temporary work for the Flag Market titled *Do You?*, in front of the Harris Museum & Art Gallery, facilitated by Bob Martin, then Arts Education Officer at Garth Prison and the Harris, where James Green was Exhibitions Officer.

A further ten years later, and after having worked together on a number of public projects in the city, including *Interruptions*,[2] James and I met in our lunch breaks to discuss how we were going to respond to the news that the imminent Tithebarn scheme – which didn't include any policy for public art – was about to start its design process.[3] The last 23 years have enabled me to develop a far greater relationship with the place than I had on my first one-day visit 33 years ago. Over that time I have slowly researched the history of the place, as I wanted to get a grasp and gain a better understanding of how it functions – architecturally, socially and politically – which I have achieved in part by physical immersion, walking the city on foot while referencing maps and archive photographs, but more so through conversations.

Preston is a city located in the North West of England on a ridge that runs north of the River Ribble. As you approach the ridge from the South along the M6 motorway (the first in the country, opened in 1958) you can see some of the tallest architectural landmarks of the city; the lantern of the neo-classical Harris Museum & Art Gallery, designed by the Preston-based architect James Hibbert, which finally opened in 1893, and the two yellow towers of Sandown Court, high-rise flats built as social housing by the Preston-based architects Building Design Partnership 70 years later, in 1963.

The town of Preston evolved along an important road that ran north from London along the ridge, and which crossed the River Ribble at its lowest point on its way to Glasgow, positioning it half-way between both major cities. It is still where Virgin train services swap staff as they travel from London's Euston Station to Scotland, with Glasgow Central Station as final destination, and vice versa, of course.

It became the first market town in the North West to gain its royal charter from Henry II in 1179, which helped establish it as a centre for trade. Preston was known regionally for its physically large market place in the thirteenth century. The town continued to develop a market economy, while becoming an administrative centre for the region, particularly with regards to lawyers and accountants. The legacy remains today, with a Session Court, a Crown Court, a Magistrate's Court and a legal community, all close to the city centre. This means that it appears on the national news channels regularly as it deals with many high-profile cases in the North West of the UK.

Pre-industrial Preston of the eighteenth and nineteenth centuries was considered a gentrified country town, complete with the Georgian Winckley Square. However, the industrial revolution saw Preston expand rapidly, having 40 mills in its heyday, which were mainly cotton mills. It was during this time that it acquired some major architectural sites, including the now Grade I listed Harris Museum & Art Gallery, as well as the Covered Market sheds, and the now demolished Gothic revivalist Town Hall, designed by Sir Gilbert Scott, who was also responsible for London's St. Pancras Station.

Preston has always been good at adapting and reinventing itself, and once the textile industry fell into decline after World War I, its

other industries – engineering and manufacturing – continued to develop, with British Electric later becoming BAE systems, which now designs and manufactures military aircrafts, including unmanned drones.

Preston has certainly not been immune to the ups and downs of the UK's national fortunes. By the 1960s central government set out to create a New Town in the Preston Chorley and Leyland area, which was followed by the forming of the Central Lancashire Development Corporation in 1971. It was the largest of the English New Towns, covering 35,255 acres.[4] Its legacy included investment into infrastructure and housing surrounding Preston, and improvements to its transport connectivity with the rest of the country. This has helped make the surrounding areas of Preston economically productive, with new housing developments, business parks and out-of-town shopping centres boosting jobs, but with as an unfortunate side effect that its city centre has been in decline ever since.

Preston had aspirations to be a city since the mid-nineteenth century, and finally, after a number of attempts, it succeeded in 2002, when it became a Jubilee City as part of Queens Elizabeth's II fiftieth jubilee celebrations. It is reported to have achieved its city status as a result of its history, location, university, diversity of its ethnicity, and being the administrative centre for Lancashire. It was still a small city, or one of 26 mid-sized cities in England with a political population of 130,000, and a wider economic population of 350,000. A year after it gained city status, Preston was able to make public its plans to work in partnership with Grosvenor Ltd. to create the Tithebarn development, which would transform a third of the city centre providing it with a modern retail and leisure complex with shops, cinemas, restaurants and residential accommodation. Preston felt it needed that other twenty-first-century industry, retail, so it could compete with its neighbours. Preston saw this as an opportunity to regenerate its city centre and to become the third city of the North West, a straightforward economic aspiration – if somewhat flawed as a city identity, and a marketing company's worst nightmare.

It was against this background that James Green, then Programmes Manager at the Harris Museum & Art Gallery, and myself, then Senior Lecturer at the University of Central Lancashire, formed In Certain Places in 2003. As far as we were aware there were no plans for public art to feature in the Tithebarn scheme. Our initial aim was to try and influence the Planning and Regeneration Departments of Preston City Council and the developer Grosvenor Ltd., who were at the time also working on the Liverpool One development, which was ahead of the Tithebarn scheme. We decided that we could achieve this in two ways. The first was to organise a series of talks, 'Speaking of Art'. We commissioned Ian Banks, an architect and public art consultant, to curate the first nine. His approach of inviting a speaker who would then invite another speaker, whom they then introduced, exposed the city to eighteen different sets of ideas and approaches in a short amount of time. Among them were for example 'Grand Gestures: The Temporary Spectacle in Public Art', presented by Lewis Biggs, then Chief Executive of the Liverpool Biennial, and Clive Gillman, artist. This series of talks was an attempt to build a critical

mass of people in the city that would be interested in the intersection of public art and urban design, which it did well to some extent by attracting design professionals, academics as well as artists. We also asked visiting speakers to talk to council officers at Town Hall during lunch. An unexpected offshoot was that after speakers visited the city (including our tours), they would spread the word about In Certain Places when back in their own locales. With the support of Ian Banks, James and I also lobbied for a Public Art Officer, who would be situated in the Planning Department, with Neil Harris taking up the post of Development Manager for Art in Public Places.

The second element was the 'Here and Now' programme, the idea of which was to commission artists to create temporary works of public art for the city. James Green, Lindsay Tayor, then Exhibitions Officer at the Harris, and I were all aware of the artist, architect and film-maker Alfredo Jaar, and in particular his project *The Skoghall Konstall* (2000) in Sweden.[5] Jaar, who lived and worked in New York, was invited to visit Preston, initially with a view to undertake a temporary commission in the city as part of the 'Here and Now' programme. However, during the course of this three-day visit it became clear that he might be able to support our work in embedding artists in the forthcoming Tithebarn project more directly. We discussed the importance that advocacy work would play in encouraging, developers, planners, master-planners and architects to embrace our proposals. As a result we agreed to finance a lecture and seminar in Preston, which Alfredo would present to key stakeholders in the project in November 2003.[6] This event proved to be more effective than any of us could have imagined, and in essence transformed the attitude of key players from passive listeners to active supporters of our proposals. Following this event, proposals for a lead artists role were developed by Alfredo Jaar, James Green and myself. This in effect promoted us into a position of actually having to work with the project's major partners at an early stage. By gaining the support from Terry Farrell architects, who were originally involved as lead architects, the idea was accepted by Grosvenor Ltd. and Preston City Council, and we were able to secure funding through the Project – Visionary Awards Scheme, which enabled us to appoint Alfredo Jaar as lead artist for the entire Tithebarn scheme.[7]

The role was meant to contribute to the master-planning process and advocate further roles for artists over the duration of the project's redevelopment. However, by the time the stage-1 planning application was submitted, which we did not have any input in, and after many public presentations and meetings with Terry Farrell architects, and later Building Design Partnership (who took over as scheme architects), it became evident that they were only paying lip service to our involvement. We were like the other shiny baubles that many regeneration schemes promoted at the beginning, and then jettisoned as hard economics kicked in. If they – the project developers – were not going to work with Terry Farrell, they certainly wouldn't be working with Alfredo Jaar and Charles Quick.

Preston has always had a sense of ambition that is disproportionate to its size, and this has continued to the present day. On reflection, the £700 million Tithebarn scheme was just

more evidence of this level of ambition. Why this is the case is hard to fathom. It could be that the city feels the need to try and match itself with its much larger neighbours of Manchester and Liverpool, or maybe it is more about its place in the geography to the north and west and east of Lancashire. There are many examples that demonstrate that, the most recent in the news being Preston Bus Station, which has now finally been listed and which was built in 1969 as the largest in Britain, if not Europe, with 80 bays.

The Victorians were known for a similar sense of ambition and left many permanent markers, including St. Walburge's church spire, which at 94 metres is in the UK only exceeded by Salisbury and Norwich cathedrals' spires. When it was built in 1892, the Albert Edward Dock was the largest single dock in Britain, joining onto the tidal River Ribble. The course of the river was moved to build the dock, with access to the river via a lock. The first roll-on roll-off, or RORO ferry as it became known, began operation in 1948, which led to the larger operation of container transport of goods, which now operates worldwide. This sense of ambition has not been restricted to architectural and engineering projects: the University of Central Lancashire is the fifth largest in the country, based on student numbers. My favourite 'feat', however, is Mrs. French scent bottle collection, which is deposited in the Harris Museum & Art Gallery, and is the largest in the UK.

The industrialisation of Preston in the nineteenth century, which led to a substantial increase in the population, certainly produced a climate in which new social ideas could flourish. Preston was the first place where the Mormons

(Church of Jesus Christ of Latter Day Saints) preached in Britain in 1837, and where they conducted mass baptisms in the River Ribble. Social change also manifested itself in sports. Preston North End FC, co-founders of the English Football League in 1888, and the first English football champions, was the first club in the county to sign a black footballer, Arthur Wharton, in 1886. It also had one of the earliest and most famous women's football teams in England: Dick Kerr's Ladies Football team was in existence from 1917 until 1965. They defeated a French team in 1920 by 2-0, which is credited as the first international women's football game. Whether the embracing of new foods is a sign of social change or not, the first KFC chicken meals served in Britain were from a restaurant on Preston's high street in 1965. Infrastructure has always been an important reason for the continued economic growth of the city, beginning with its place on an early route, followed by developments in its river, canal and rail transport. In 1958 the first section of the M6 motorway was built to bypass Preston.

What is it about this mid-sized city that has generated such ambition and so many new ideas and firsts? Is it the geography or the people that inhabit it, or does everywhere have a list of firsts? Our experience of Preston is that it is a receptive place if you want to test something. It is surprisingly open to new ideas and there is a willingness to try things out for the first time. In recent times this has meant its public spaces, which have survived the Tithebarn retail regeneration scheme, have been allowed to be animated by projects as diverse as a drive-in cinema in the Covered Market (led by They Eat Culture and the AND festival),

a large-scale Passion play using the Preston Bus Station forecourt as one of its stage sets (broadcast by the BBC), and the *Harris Flights* on the Flag Market commissioned by In Certain Places, and not forgetting the Guild celebrations that populated many public and private spaces in the city.

Is this the beginning of a culture-led regeneration of the city centre, supported by the recent adoption by Preston City Council of a cultural framework? Some would argue that culture alone cannot offer sustainable regeneration. A lot has been written about culture-led regeneration, a popular example being Liverpool with its Biennial, which first took place in 1999, and which is said to have contributed to the city being awarded the honour of being Capital of Culture in 2008. This in turn attracted Grosvenor Ltd., which constructed the Liverpool One scheme on land given to them by Liverpool City Council. The Quays along the River Tyne, which separate Newcastle and Gateshead, are another example of regeneration, which had its foundation in the visual arts, symbols of which are not only Anthony Gormley's *Angel of the North* (1998), but also the Baltic Centre of Contemporary Art (opened in 2002) and The Sage (opened in 2004).

The important question is who all that culture is for. Or, as Steven Miles says:

> 'Perhaps then our cities (or at least the rhetoric that surrounds our cities) are in this sense unreal: more the creation of an idealised bourgeois image of what a cultural city might be than a genuine expression of what it means to live in a place.'[8]

Preston has survived a potential retail regeneration, which would have created a homogenised city-centre experience, not unlike that of Liverpool One, in architectural style and certainly with regards to the kind of shops it would have hosted. Now it has the opportunity to slowly consider a kind of regeneration that is particular to the place, its history and its people.

1. Longridge is a small town in the borough of Ribble Valley in Lancashire. It is situated at the end of Longridge Fell, a long ridge above the River Ribble, several miles northeast of Preston. The town grew from the mid-nineteenth century as cotton mills and stone quarries were opened. These have all now closed, although stone quarried in the town was used to construct the M55 motorway in the 1970s.

2. One of the first architectural interventions using light that I created was with the Harris Museum & Art Gallery and the St. Peter Church at the University of Central Lancashire This project was commissioned by Professor Lubaina Himid at UCLan and James Green at the Harris Museum & Gallery, and in some ways could be seen as a precursor to forming In Certain Places three years later. The institutions worked together to commission me to realise the work. Each building had new lights fitted, which intermittently came on and off, making the buildings appear dysfunctional across the night landscape of the city. The project was 'live' between 5pm and 1am over a period of two weeks and was called *Interruptions*.

3. In short, the Preston Tithebarn redevelopment project was a £700 million city-centre regeneration initiative, which was intended to be developed by Preston Tithebarn Partnership between Grosvenor Ltd. and Preston City Council, later including Lend Lease Corporation in a joint venture 50/50 partnership. The Grosvenor Group is a British property corporation, while Lend Lease describes itself as a 'leading, fully integrated, international property and infrastructure group.' In October 2005, Preston City Council and Grosvenor Ltd. signed an agreement to go ahead with the Tithebarn regeneration project as part of the Council's broader plans for Preston city centre. In November 2011 the scheme was abandoned after John Lewis pulled out.

4. New Towns in the UK were planned under the New Towns Act 1946 and later Acts to disperse population following World War II. They were not completely new, but developed around historic cores. Designated new towns were removed from local authority control and placed under the supervision of a Development Corporation. These Corporations were later disbanded and their assets split between local authorities and, in England, the Commission for New Towns.

5. Alfredo Jaar said about the Konsthall: 'I propose to design and build a new, contemporary structure to house the new Skoghall Konsthall. This structure will be built completely

in paper produced by the Paper Mill, in close collaboration with local architects and builders. The design will reflect the best of contemporary Swedish architecture in its minimal elegance and respect for the environment. It will also reflect the generous commitment of the main local industry in the creation of a forward-looking structure and institution that will project Skoghall into the future. The opening exhibition will feature the first exhibition ever held in Skoghall of young emerging Swedish artists from Stockholm, Malmo and Gotenburg. The Konsthall will be officially inaugurated by the Mayor of the City, in the presence of the entire local community. Exactly 24 hours after its opening, the Skoghall Konsthall will disappear, engulfed in flames. The burning of the structure will be pre-planned and will satisfy the most demanding security requirements.' See http://www.alfredojaar.net/.

6.   The press release announcing the Lead Artist scheme stated the following:

'The Lead Artist scheme is a pioneering project to employ artists in the Tithebarn masterplanning process. New York based artist Alfredo Jaar and UK artist Charles Quick have been appointed through the CABE/A&B/ACE Project – Visionary Awards Scheme to broker artist/architect partnerships from the earliest stages and to contribute to the masterplanning process as equal

partners with Grosvenor Ltd, PCC, and the urban design and architectural master planners for the scheme. The lead artist role will contribute to the masterplanning process and advocate further roles for artists over the duration of the Tithebarn redevelopment.

The involvement of the Lead Artists will be at a design team level offering new perspectives and ensuring that commissioning opportunities for other artists are integrated within the scheme from the earliest stage. Artists will be involved at all levels, from informing high level masterplanning decisions to designing building façades, street lighting and public consultation projects, which will significantly impact on the quality of the urban environment.'

7.   Project was run by Public Art South West, and was funded by CABE, Arts & Business and Arts Council England.

8.   Steven Miles, 'Small City – big ideas', in David Bell and Mark Jayne, eds., *Small Cities – Urban Experience beyond the Metropolis*, Routledge, 2006, p.241.

Summary of Initiatives to Ensure the Involvement of Artists within the Regeneration of Preston, 2004

Over the past eighteen months Preston City Council, working in partnership with the University of Central Lancashire, have developed a number of initiatives to ensure artists have a significant role in the regeneration of the city – specifically in connection with the Tithebarn redevelopment project.

These initiatives are being led by James Green, Preston City Council, and Charles Quick, University of Central Lancashire. It is envisaged the Development Manager for Art in Public Places will join this project development team working to implement these programmes.

This briefing note offers a summary of activity to date.

Background

Preston City Council and Grosvenor Limited are currently finalising a Development Agreement for the redevelopment of almost one third of Preston's existing city centre, known as the Tithebarn Project. The project will be a mixed-use redevelopment incorporating retail, leisure, cultural, business, residential and health components and will result in an investment of some £500m in the city centre.

The project will also incorporate a new bus station, a new markets quarter and wwill see a significant increase in both the quality and extent of the public realm in the city centre.

Farrell and Partners are the urban design and architectural masterplanners working on the project and the intention is to appoint a further seven architectural practices to work on the various scheme packages along with specialist landscape and environmental consultants.

The first hybrid planning application (part outline, part detail) is programmed for early 2005 with a start on site targeted for Autumn 2007.

The City Council intends to use the Tithebarn Project as a catalyst for the regeneration of the whole city, integrating cultural, social and economic aspects. Additional funding for spin-off projects is being made available from the North West Development Agency (NWDA) Single Pot Programme and the City Council has set up a Vision Board to facilitate and monitor the implementation of regeneration projects so as to add maximum value to the Tithebarn initiative.

Existing plans for the involvement of artists in the scheme

Over the past eighteen months Preston City Council, in partnership with many regional and national agencies, has developed a number of initiatives to influence the engagement of artists, at the highest level, in the city's redevelopment.

Sufficient funding has been secured to proceed with all projects and development teams are in place.

Here and Now – Temporary art for a transitional city

Between spring 2005 and 2008 the Harris Museum and Art Gallery, Preston, and the University of Central Lancashire (UCLan) will develop a programme of temporary artworks, commissioned for sites and places, predominantly in the city centre.

The programme's aims will be:

> to raise the level of debate surrounding art in public places within the city and specifically in the context of the Tithebarn development.

> to support the planning for the development of ambitious public commissions, both temporary and permanent, and high quality urban design for the Tithebarn Project.

Over £120,000 has been secured to date although we anticipate the final sum generated will be approximately £330,000.

Speaking of Art
Talks and debates informing art and architecture in Preston's regeneration

Eight events between October 2004 and June 2005. Ian Banks, architect and public art specialist, has been commissioned to develop a programme of themed lectures and debates exploring issues such as *Public Art and Regeneration; Architect as Artist as Architect; The Case for Temporary Installations; The Enlightened Client; New International Perspectives; New Media and Architecture.*

This project develops from a lecture by Alfredo Jaar, hosted by UCLan in November 2003, which was attended by some 200 individuals representing organisations keen to develop an arts agenda as a keystone to Preston's urban renaissance. In July, Terry Farrell delivered a lecture and accompanying exhibition at the Harris Museum and Art Gallery, Preston, exploring his approach to masterplanning for Preston and previous working relationship with artists.

Full funding for this programme is in place.

City Brand

As an ancillary project the City Council is working with NWDA and UCLan to identify ways in which smaller towns/cities can compete with and offer viable urban alternatives to the regional core cities, which are currently monopolising the urban regeneration agenda. The initial budget for this programme s £250,000, which is intended to provide research grants and additional teaching facilities within the design faculty at UCLan, aimed at creating a new persona for the City of Preston.

A major factor in this scheme is the embodiment of quality art and design at all levels of the city's redevelopment process and its integration at the earliest possible stages of each project.

A Lead Artist role for Tithebarn

Both Grosvenor and the City Council are keen to appoint a Lead Artist to work alongside the masterplan architects to develop concepts and programmes at all levels throughout the schemes, from identifying opportunities for the integration of artists' 'work' into the basic fabric of the Tithebarn Project and brokering artist/architect partnerships, to informing higher level masterplanning decisions.

Sir Terry Farrell, the masterplan architect, is fully supportive of this initiative, having been involved in similar (though smaller scale) work with Liam Gillick on the Home Office redevelopment project in Marsham Street, London.

Artist Alfredo Jaar has, in principle, agreed to take on the role of Lead Artist to contribute to the Tithebarn masterplanning process and to develop new initiatives involving artists in the further development of the Tithebarn scheme. In order to address logistical issues surrounding his involvement (Jaar is based in New York), and in order to take advantage of other's experience, Jaar will work

in partnership with the UK artist Charles Quick. Quick has considerable experience of working in the public realm in the UK and important local knowledge and experience.

Jaar and Quick's approach will result in artists' involvement in many aspects of the scheme and will result in artists' contributions being integral to the project's development and final manifestation. For example an artist may be commissioned to address lighting across the scheme, aspects of public consultation or street signage, all of which have existing budget allocations.

Jaar and Quick's role will be as full participants and partners in the ongoing process, including involvement in all levels of decision-making and as participants in regular design team meetings and at other levels as becomes appropriate

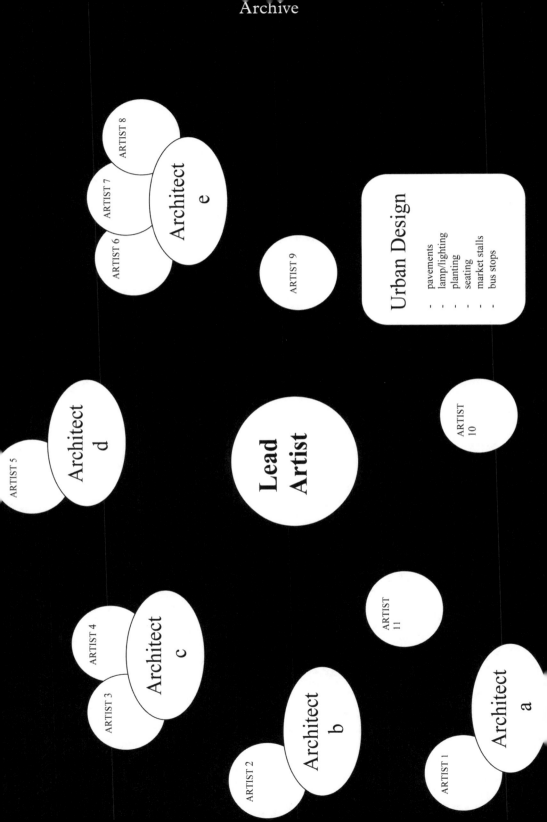

James Green

I started at the Harris in 1989 and always enjoyed projects that would resonate with the rest of the building and the collections. We would do lots of projects where artists would come in and do interventions with the social history collection, or made gallery-based exhibitions that responded to perhaps a more curious aspect of the collections. Around 1998 I became interested in doing a project that responded to the Harris building. That project was called the 'Harris Museum Project'. We wanted to commission eight or nine artists to respond to the building's form, history or function. It became a more longitudinal programme that ran over seven years. We finished with Simon Starling, which must have been around 2003.

What was really key was that we ended up doing projects outside the gallery spaces. We did the project with Keith Wilson, which was early 2000s. He had developed a string of projects, which happened simultaneously, some of them tiny little interventions, mixed into displays in various parts of the building. His proposal was poetic: he wanted to create a puddle in the Market Square that involved taking up six flag stones and relaying them in such a way that, should it rain, a puddle would temporarily form. If you wanted to see it as an artwork, you could come and seek it out, and if it had been raining, there it would be. If you hadn't picked up the marketing material, and you weren't the kind of person who would seek these things out, then it would

look like every other ten square yards of the Market Square. We then went through this process of negotiating this piece of work, which involved conversations with Health and Safety people and the Works Department. Inevitably these negotiations became the work, and went on for a long time. For such a long time that we ended up promoting the project before we had final permission. In the end the Head of Technical Services made a decision that he couldn't allow it to happen. He was protecting councillors, the elected members, from reputational damage.

Keith was fantastically well connected, so we had a great number of letters of support from people like critic Sacha Craddock, saying 'Keith, we're really looking forward to seeing it'. In the end the story was picked up by *The Guardian*. The journalist Miranda Sawyer came up and wrote a four-page piece in magazine called 'Wet Dreams'. It recounted the story of this project that went nowhere, with the negotiation and trying to get permission even more ridiculous than the actual work itself. The week after the feature came out there was a senior management meeting, and they were all there with their fresh copies of *The Guardian* in front of them! Alex Walker (Head of Arts and Heritage) really did support it, she wasn't going to back down or apologise for it.

Puddle led to an idea that the gallery should be doing more things about the public realm and what public art might be. The next stage was having a conversation with Peter Robertson, the Dean of what is now the School of Art, Design and Performance at UCLan. At the time someone in the marketing department of the university had been proposing a string of commissions between the university and the city centre, along Friargate. There was also a lot of discussion about town and gown, and the university trying to get a bit more of a civic profile. So the idea that the Harris might start to do something off-site was resonating with what the university was interested in. When Charles got involved, the project developed into something much different.

Getting involved with the Tithebarn scheme comprised three elements; a lead artist, who had a master-planning role, a programme of public lectures, and a commissioning programme. The thinking behind this three-pronged approach was that all commissioning happens within a public context, and history dictates that there is an element of public consultation and a process of agreement. It seems very unfair to ask a public that doesn't have very good models to draw on to comment on what they want to see. So the idea of this temporary commissions programme was to present a series of experimental and different models. The lecture programme disseminated ideas and we would all be learning at the same time about things that might be possible and things that might work. The first masterplan was done by architect Terry Farrell, who was really interested in the idea of working with artists.

Alfredo Jaar came and did a session in Preston. It was an astonishing event, where he did a slide presentation that was about an hour long. He had two slide projectors and projected these images of public art all over the world and he talked about some of his work, and others' work and very gently mentioned different approaches. He was like a guru. The event turned more people who were slightly sceptical on to the possibility of something.

The idea with the Jeppe Hein work – the first commission in the temporary public art programme – was that it was like a labyrinth; you would step into one square and then the water would drop, then step into another square, and gradually you would get through it without getting wet. Not in Preston! It was amazing, kids going in, in their school uniforms in the morning. That piece still has currency though. The council wanted it extended, but Charles was very good at saying, 'I think we should finish it when people want more.'

Some people in galleries see their responsibility as all about the programme and all about what happens inside of the building. I think that galleries have a real responsibility to their communities and their towns. There are massive opportunities, in Penzance [Green is now Director at Newlyn Art Gallery and The Exchange], we've started using the gallery as a forum of discussion for the town, rather than being a massively overbearing presence of art or artists. There will be a point where we start introducing artists to those discussions. Some people may see that as being a very complicated and weird thing; but having worked with Elaine and Charles, it seems very straightforward. It's open to challenge, but those projects seem so much more interesting than an encounter with a piece of work in a gallery.

Even if it doesn't work, at least you've shown that. Whether it's adapting and developing it or just discounting it, you go through a process of change and testing. I think it energises people; it's new, so they don't get a chance to become bored with it, and it encourages people to think creatively. People don't feel like it is being imposed upon them, it's something they can use and interact with. There's been a journey that's got us to where we are now, where something like the *Harris Flights* doesn't frighten people as much as it would have done five or six years ago.

By making somewhere interesting, lots of other good things will happen. I think that's part of the advantage of these In Certain Places events. It's about allowing some of that debate to happen. I can see it in discussions we have at work. People are interested in where we could go next and want to do something creative, not just sit back and wait for Grosvenor or whoever to do something. There's an understanding that there are some smaller-scale actions that we can take, which will nudge things along. But you do need that creative and collaborative approach to move a city forward.

Nigel Roberts,
Principal Urban Designer,
Preston City Council

If you talk about In Certain Places as a public art initiative, it means a certain thing to a lot of people – it means 'look at this shiny thing in the middle of the city', that's what often comes to mind. That's what a lot of these big arts organisations are after. But the projects that you do can be as grand as the *Harris Flights*, or as sneaky as running around town at 8am, trying and get into empty buildings and taping them up. So I think there are different ways that you approach things.

It's good to have one platform where funny, little activist projects can share the same space as, for example, Magda Stawarska-Beavan's beautiful sound piece or something as massive as Jeppe Hein's *Appearing Rooms*. The project is really open to totally different ideas, finding value in different things and not being afraid of projects that are a bit political and push people's buttons.

Steph Fletcher,
Artist

Amplifying Civic Space
Charles Quick

When In Certain Places installed Jeppe Hein's interactive water work *Appearing Rooms* in its all but forgotten historic Preston Market Square during six weeks of the hot summer of 2006, we could not foresee what the artist would unlock by his decision to use that space. The piece became a vehicle for revisiting that site, questioning how people saw it, and how it could be used in the future. It began a dialogue with the city about its public spaces that moved between the temporary to the permanent and back again.

Henry II awarded the town its first royal charter in 1179, enabling it to become a regional centre for market trade. By 1250 it had the largest market space in the North West after it decided to demolish a field of burgage plots with buildings facing onto Church street.[1] This space has remained as the town's market square ever since, becoming known as the Flag Market. Through it, Preston's identity in medieval England was established.

Looking at Preston's Flag Market today it's possible to see and understand all its histories and forms on its journey from market square to that of primary civic space. Our understanding of these different functions and identities can be linked to the Greek Agora, which was created as a space for civic functions and the political life of the city, later including markets. In Preston, the Flag Market began life as a commercial space and later became that civic space, a process that was largely driven by the guilds of the town.

Jeppe Hein's intervention was presented at a time when in the UK nationally-funded regional development agencies were very present, converging with a desire to regenerate urban landscapes by reviving them, or, as some saw it, by creating new public civic places. Places Matter! produced a guide for the creation of a high-quality public realm, entitled 'Creating Inspirational Spaces'.[2] It was full of examples of newly created civic spaces, often incorporating water and fountains. Piccadilly Gardens in Manchester, for instance, featured a large fountain that was opened in 2002, in the build-up to the Commonwealth Games.

Across the Pennines in Yorkshire, Leeds created a new civic space from demolished land and the reuse of a small city-centre park. Millennium Square, completed in 2001, gave a central identity to an area described as the new civic quarter. John Thorp, until recently Leeds's Civic Architect, talks about 'seeking inspiration from such renowned spaces as the Piazza San Marco in Venice and the Campo in Siena' – a market place established before the thirteenth century.[3] Piazza del Campo was built on a slope and has a footprint that has only been slightly modified over time. These Mediterranean spaces grew over hundreds of years and relied on the surrounding architecture for their particularity historic importance, and the question that raises is whether we could look at UK cities and approach our city squares in similar ways.

Preston's response was to organise an international competition in partnership with the Landscape Institute in 2008, leading to six shortlisted proposals for the redesign of the Flag Market.[4] Water featured in many and all would have completely changed the space. However, the selection of the winning submission, in 2009, coincided with the worldwide economic collapse, followed by political change, which resulted in the disbanding of the regional development agency, and the cutting of finance for the realisation of the project in its entirety.

The Urban Design and Planning Department of Preston City Council used the winning design, by Landscape Projects, Research Design and myself, as inspiration for their more modest remodelling of the space. The result has been that some of the trees were removed from Market Square, which opened up the space and revived the vista from the front of Harris Museum & Art Gallery along Friargate. Their adapted approach has also introduced new seating and trees, and led to the renovation of the entire square's paving.

Preston City Council also recognised the contribution that In Certain Places and artists had made to the process and invited them to contribute to the Heritage Lottery Fund supported 'Preston Remembers' scheme, aimed at restoring and remodelling the listed Cenotaph, designed by the architect Sir Gilbert Scott – a work that is seen by many as one of the most important pieces of memorial architecture of its time in Britain. One of the initial ways

in which In Certain Places contributed to the debate around the process was by organising the symposium 'The Monument and the Changing City', during which artists, academics and architects spoke about what a monument in a city could be in the twenty-first century. Subsequently it commissioned two artists, Laurence Payot and Jenny Steele, who conducted research that engaged the public in sharing how they navigated and understood the market space and the Cenotaph, producing drawings, photographs and films.

This space had retained its original footprint up to the Victorian era, when objects contained within it, and its boundaries began to change. The market cross, originally erected in 1782, was removed in 1858, and stored until 1979, when it was returned to Market Square. The memorial to soldiers who died in the Boer War, which was unveiled at the beginning of the twentieth century, was later moved to Avenham Park, when the Cenotaph was built in its place in 1926.

The Victorians and Edwardians created the grander version of the civic space as we know it today; by demolishing the existing buildings that surrounded it and replacing them with administrative buildings. Over a period of 50 years, the scale of the architecture that surrounded the square grew to what we can consider as civic proportions. The process started with the construction of Sir George Gilbert Scott's Gothic Town Hall, in 1855, which was to be replaced in the 1960s by the most inappropriately named building in the city: Crystal House. In direct competition to the Town Hall was James Hibbert's neo-classical Free Public Library and Museum, now named after its benefactor as the Harris Museum & Art Gallery, which opened in 1894. The Italianate Miller Arcade, a prime retail and leisure outlet, was opened in the 1890s, with the Edwardian Baroque Sessions House and separate Post Office both being in place by 1903. Finally Cheapside, on the west-side of Market Square, was on the whole left alone and still has a footprint that references the burgage plots that had been there since the 1200s.

Over time the Flag Market has slowly become more important as a place for civic ceremony, public celebrations, and political demonstrations, the one constant event to be programmed in that space being the Preston Guild, a once in a generation (every 20 years) event. It has been celebrated since the royal charter in 1179, originally as a way of reaffirming the right for the burgage tenants to continue trading in the town. The contemporary Guild lasts over a week and comprises many events, including four large street processions. In 2012 Iain Broadley created *The Black Parade*, which was one of 126 floats to take part in the Community Parade in front of 60,000 spectators, and which also took part in the Torchlight Parade. Both events enabled the concerns and participants of the project to be centre stage on the Flag Market. More recently, that same space saw the Save Preston Bus Station parade finish its procession through the city with speeches and performances.

Eight years after In Certain Places' first commission for Market Square, the city now has an extremely functional and more authoritative civic space in front of its very impressive Grade I listed building of the Harris

Museum & Art Gallery. It does not have water features or landscaping that would interfere with events or ceremonies. Instead objects have been moved to its edges. The most symbolic movement of an object has been that of the market cross, which now sits on the south-side of the space, having given up its prominent position in the centre. Opposite it, on the north-side, now stands the recently reworked and renovated Cenotaph, which has given the space a different emphasis. Remembrance Sunday in November is only one example of the ceremonial use of the square. Many other events use the plinth of the Harris as their focal point, as if it were the front of a Town Hall, including the reading of the Guild Scrolls every 20 years, or the addressing of the crowds by local celebrities, politicians and royalty. The Flag Market now is almost the Harris's patio. The building's architect, James Hibbert, would have been very pleased with that.

This relationship between the space and the architecture was explored very explicitly in the summer of 2013 by the architectural intervention of the *Harris Flights,* created by architect Charlie MacKeith and myself. The structure allowed the people of Preston for the first time direct access from the square to the front door of the building, also providing the infrastructure for performances and spectators over a four-week period. The influence of this most recent commission and intervention will perhaps be seen in future years, following the debates it has begun; about the lack of visibility of the side entrances to the museum for first-time visitors, and the (rising) level of ambitions for future festivals in Preston's many public spaces.

Introduction

1. A concept dating back to medieval times, burgage plots were a form of tenure by which land or property in a town was held in return for service or annual rent.

2. Places Matter! is an organisation devoted to generating a strong sense of place in living, working and leisure environments throughout the UK's North West. For more information see http://www.placesmatter.co.uk.

3. John Thorp, *From the Tile to the City. A journey through civic architecture and the design in the city of Leeds*, Leeds City Council, 2012. John Thorp retired from his position as Leeds Civic Architect, the last such position in the UK, in March 2014.

4. The Landscape Institute is the Royal Chartered institute for landscape architects, a professional umbrella and membership organisation, in the UK. For more information see http://www.landscapeinstitute.co.uk/.

Amplifying Civic Space

The thing that really sticks in my mind is the first big intervention by Jeppe Hein, the fountain. I thought it was really exciting; it changed the way Prestonians used Preston and thought about the city centre. Whether they were there because it was fun, or because of a deeper meaning, it transformed the cultural institutions that shared the square. I had been sitting inside this big cultural box that is the Harris, which is a fantastic place, but it felt quite internal. So suddenly that institution, along with UCLan, could begin to influence the way in which people used the city. It really opened up the horizon for what the Harris might be able to do in the future. I remember that being really exciting and recently the *Harris Flights* have had the same effect. These projects bookend the last decade for me, in the context of In Certain Places. They really changed how people thought of Preston and how they use the city.

Richard Smith, former Assistant Exhibitions Officer at the Harris Museum & Art Gallery

We want to change people's relationships with the city centre, so that they see it as a place to come and enjoy events together. We want to build on the way that the *Harris Flights* encourages people to spend time in the Flag Market – having lunch on the steps, or meeting friends – to develop the space as a social hub.

People enjoy sitting at the top of the steps and on the platform of the Harris, which provides a vista of the city that you don't usually get to see. The project has sparked debate around how people enter the Harris, and there will be a desire for it to be made permanent, which we saw with the fountain that In Certain Places provided [Jeppe Hein's *Appearing Rooms* in 2006]. These things have a big impact and benefit a lot of people. I think the debate around the benefits that the *Flights* have brought to the Harris and the Flag Market will continue long after the project is finished.

Tim Joel, Events Manager, Preston City Council

I've already met people who say that they wish that the *Harris Flights* were staying permanently, and that the transformation of the city centre it's bringing about is something that should happen all the time. So I think that it will engender a debate about how we use that really great space in the middle of the city. This is a great example of how you can create a really active and dynamic public performance space.

Physically it's an area that much of the time is empty, and through this project we have turned it into a space that's full of activity, and that people are coming to a lot more than normal. So, for a temporary period the city centre is being regenerated. The real question is how to build on that.

Prof. Rod Dubrow-Marshall, former Pro-vice Chancellor UCLan

Jeppe Hein, *Appearing Rooms*, Preston Market Square

Appearing Rooms is an interactive sculpture by the Danish artist Jeppe Hein, which was installed in Preston's Market Square for six weeks during the summer of 2006. The sculpture radically transformed the nature of the space from a thoroughfare and shortcut to other locations in the city, to a place in which people chose to spend time and interact. *Appearing Rooms* was especially popular with families, many of whom travelled from outside of Preston to visit the work, armed with towels and swimming costumes.

June–July 2006

Splashing start

GREAT FUN: Left, Sarah Nash, six, playing in the water fountain Right, the scenes on the Flag Market

prestontoday.net for video footage

ACTION ONLINE

PRESTON'S big arts festival was given a boost with the launch of an amazing water feature on the city's Flag Market.

Organised by the Arts Council England North West and Preston Council, art06 is the third annual spotlight on the region's arts.

Today the fish market section of the outdoor market was being transformed in a cultural arena.

Preston is following in the footsteps of Liverpool and Manchester in hosting the event which will see the city's streets lined with arts-

The market was featuring a packed programme of free events including the latest from over 60 arts organisations between 10am and 5pm. Members of the public were able to see live performances and other community-led music projects.

And yesterday the event was given a flying start with the opening of Jeppe Hein's stunning open air water sculpture on the Flag Market.

Hein's water feature, Appearing Rooms, is also part of the Here + Now programme

range of projects, each exploring differ- approaches to public commissioning.

The aim is to explore ways artists can tribute to the shaping of the city.

At today's event all types of art were show, with the day culminating in an award party to celebrate arts in the North West. A arts-based debate was taking place betwe 3.30pm and 5pm at the Harris Museum, fe turing playwright David Edgar and thea company boss Jatinder Verma. It will broadcast on Radio Three at 9.30pm Monday.

Meanwhile, the Minster of St John Church Street was being used for art-ce tred debates for people with a commerc

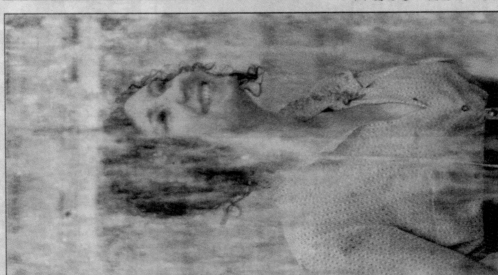

ET LOOK: Nicola Ellis, 19, in the water fountain on Pre-

In Certain Places and Research Design, *Harris Flights,* Preston Market Square

In Certain Places worked with architectural practice Research Design to examine the original plans for the Harris Museum & Art Gallery, drawn up by architect James Hibbert, and to create a new temporary staircase, which invited people to move directly from the space of Preston's Market Square into the heart of the Harris building. The *Flights* took people through the 'front door' of the building on the first floor, allowing them to experience the neo-classical, Grade I listed building in an entirely new way.

The project emphasised the relationship between the front of the Harris Museum and the Market Square in which it sits. Standing in the square, individuals can feel architecturally divorced from the interior of the museum. However, by taking people straight up and into the building, the *Flights* increased museum visits by 70 per cent. Moreover, there has been local debate about whether the original design for the building included steps, and the difficulty of navigating the entrance. This is coupled with a desire to create wider access to the podium, which has been a focus for ceremonial occasions, and a vantage point for important visitors, such as kings and queens, prime ministers, football teams and celebrities, to address the people below. *Harris Flights* was designed to extend opportunities for all people to see the city from what has previously been the viewpoint of a privileged few.

The *Flights* also became a new destination in the city centre: a space to 'hang out' and a cultural hub for performances, contemporary art installations, workshops, demonstrations and talks by artists and university and community groups. It was a stage for an audience to spectate from the Market Square, and, at other times, a stadium from which to view events below. During the four weeks of its installation, over 60 events were organised on and around the *Flights*.

August–September 2013

Step in the right direction for festival

By RACHEL HURST
rachel.hurst@lep.co.uk
@REAL_RACHELH

TO the untrained eye, it was merely a set of steps... but the Harris Flights will live long in the memory of Prestonians for years to come.

The month long festival of music, arts and dance came to a close at the weekend with a cinema on the steps, Caribbean festival and outdoor theatre.

Among the dancers, artists and performers was a University of Central Lancashire (UCLan) lecturer, William Titley, who ran a marathon 26 miles up and down the temporary staircase around the Harris Museum, an Aspic Jelly Parade and big screenings of favourite movies such as Some Like It Hot and Ghostbusters.

Councillor Tom Burns from Preston City Council said: "On the whole the Harris Flights were a great success.

"I went every weekend and there was always something really interesting going on.

"This is the first time we have done anything like this and we plan to do more cultural programmes such as this in the future.

"The flights really drew people into the museum and it was so good to see so many families going into see the exhibits at the Harris and getting involved with the interactive displays.

"There are things that we can take from the success of the flights. Things we can use in the near future to enhance the city centre even further for visitors coming into Preston."

SHOWTIME: The screening of Ghostbusters on the Harris Flights

BIG ATTRACTION: The Unpicking Aspic Jellies Parade. To view video of these events visit www.lep.co.uk PICTURES: Ian Robin

MARATHON MAN: William Titley, a Fine Art lecturer from UCLan running a marathon on the Harris flights and around the museum

STRANGE BREW: Olivia Keith in the Unpicking Aspic Jellies Parade

BUMPER CROWD: The festival was well supported

Amplifying Civic Space

This made people aware that art is
more than paintings or statues, and
many people became involved with
it who would probably not think of
going into an art gallery. This was
clear because of the enquiries we had
and the number of people using it.
It brought the art to the people.

> Tourist Information
> Centre Manager

A positive contribution to the
sense of place and vibrancy of
the Flag Market.

> Preston City Council Principal
> Landscape Architect

Excellent! It enlivened the square
and brought some real vitality to the
city centre. It is exactly what should
be happening more often in Preston.

> Preston City Council Planning
> Policy Manager

One of the things that attracted us
to this particular project was the
ability to have multiple events taking
place. So you have this temporary
structure that provides you with an
opportunity to bring in professionally
organised events from outside, as
well as for the community to use. It's
a real opportunity for them to perform
or do whatever they want to. Critically,
it is called the *Harris Flights*, and one
of the exciting things is that it draws
you into the Harris Museum.

> Lorraine Norris, Chief Executive,
> Preston City Council

Preston Remembers, Preston Market Square

During the summer of 2012, artists Jenny Steele and Laurence Payot examined how the Market Square is used, and how Prestonians relate to the Cenotaph, which sits within it. Collectively, Payot and Steele traced people's movements, looked for visual patterns in chaotic and constant flows, photographed, categorised and created mock-ups of the space, encouraged people to re-imagine the Cenotaph and draw their own journeys, and created animations about the space.

Their research informed Preston City Council's 'Preston Remembers' project, which was funded by the Heritage Lottery Fund. The project has renovated and remodelled the Cenotaph reflecting much of Sir Giles Gilbert Scott's original design.

Jenny Steele, *Following the Market Square*

Following the Market Square was a multi-layered project, through which Steele interacted with people online and across the city to explore their engagement with the Cenotaph and Market Square. Her research included a short residency at the Harris Museum & Art Gallery, during which she invited people who use the square to contribute to a collaborative drawing and to express their perceptions of the existing square and war memorial. She also tracked people's movements across the space in a hand-drawn animation entitled *Observation of Desire Lines*.

August 2012

It's huge, obvious but yet obscure and hidden: A space that is taken for granted.

Laurence Payot,
Supervised and *From My Eyes*

Payot spent a day photographing the Market Square and categorised the resulting photographs as the basis for a series of mock-up images. Laurence explains: 'The categorising technique I used is very similar to the one used in monitoring forms, where we become a tick in a box, but transforming it into a visual form makes it look strangely humorous (some of the images look like they could be of a performance or an event), as well as ironically dark and sectarian.'

For the second stage of her research, *From My Eyes*, the artist sought to discover people's perceptions of the Cenotaph by asking them to draw the monument and make their own additions to it. The images were then edited to create an animation, which gives a collective life to the still and quiet monument.

August 2012

The Monument and the Changing City

'The Monument and the Changing City' symposium was a day-long event, which examined issues of collective memory and the city, through presentations by Paul Gough, Charles Quick, Jonathan Vickery, Chris Meigh-Andrews, Lubaina Himid and Alan Rice. It explored the impact, purpose and aesthetic merit of public commemorative and memorial works from across the world, and the role of public memory within the changing city.

The event included a tour, led by Charlie MacKeith, of Preston's Cenotaph, which was designed by Sir Giles Gilbert Scott. MacKeith explained the design development of Gilbert Scott's memorials in the Market Square and the Harris Museum, between 1919 and 1926, in the context of the national search for appropriate commemoration of the sacrifice of so many during World War I. Due to vague central government recommendations, communities produced varied responses specific to unique, local demands. Using examples of Scott's design drawings, the tour explained how one of Britain's leading architects developed a language of commemoration for Preston, which, in addition to the memorials, gave the world one of Britain's most iconic symbols.

March 2011

Art, Urban Publics and the City
Jonathan Vickery

What role do In Certain Places play in the public realm? Understanding the 'art' of In Certain Places requires understanding the dynamics of their work in the public realm of a particular city: Preston. They grapple with one of the central cultural issues of our time: how we put art to work in the city. The UK has seen four decades of impressive public art *exhibited* in our cities, made for a 'viewing' public or an 'audience', usually in pre-designated spaces provided by urban planners, architects and urban designers. Even contemporary art exhibitions are now a regular feature of city life, and can attract 'blockbuster' crowds. Yet, a question remains: how can we put art to work in the re-making of the city itself? Outside the socially selective spheres of institutions and galleries, how can art create a space in which the people of a city encounter their city as a vital question?

In Certain Places are driven by the intellectual leadership of artist-academics, Charles Quick and Elaine Speight, but not dominated by their work. They commission and engage with a wide range of practitioners, including Katja van Driel and Wouter Osterholt, Iain Broadley, Shezad Dawood, Teresa and Dominique Hodgson-Holt, Martin Hamblen and Leo Fitzmaurice, among many others. With all of them, the critical function of artistic culture in the city is a consistent theme. The city is not simply a backdrop, plinth or urban 'stage', but often the subject, content and medium of art, where it investigates the streets, the shops, market or memorial spaces, and in so doing establishes the 'right' of art to the city, and the role of art in forming a space for urban public culture.

Everyday urban culture is something lived, not often an object of reflection. It is common knowledge how environment and habitus form a young person's horizon of expectations, social aspiration and sensible openness to a world of possibility. Cities are the spaces in which cultural, social and industrial modernity emerged; they are equally the places where crucial movements of political and intellectual emancipation were born. This is not incidental, and draws our attention to the vital material conditions for self-generated change embedded in the urban environment. The art of In Certain Places opens a series of temporary spaces, which in turn use art as a means of both reflection and motivation for social exploration of the city.

Walking down the high streets of Preston, while one encounters the still impressive world of industrial modernity, it is bereft of the living particularity of regional and local trade, produce and tastes. The spaces between the historical remainder are animated by the 'place-less' fasciae of global brands and the products of a global market homogeneity, found in any city.

Since the 1990s, urban theorists have referred to the contemporary British city as an 'entrepreneurial city' or 'neo-liberal city'.[1] Urban regeneration was a central public policy mechanism through which city municipalities became command and control centres for the 'urban economy', where 'economy' was understood as supply and consumption in the context of a global marketplace.[2] The 'economy' became a dominant political discourse whereby the city (from government to culture) was re-cast as a business hub and platform for capital. Forever destined to live in a state of craving for commerce and for Foreign Direct Investment (FDI), the cultural sector benefited in terms of unprecedented public funding and new facilities. The implications of this change, however, soon emerged in the form of the sale of public assets, property commodification and rise of basic rental costs, foreign ownership and absentee landlords, hedge-fund-owned buildings, global-brand-driven shopping centres and once-open public space now privatised and security-protected. New forms of social segregation emerged with a new priority of commercial over civic uses of city space, and gradually local- and regionally-owned business, trade and non-monetary micro-economies declined.[3] Prime urban space gradually morphed around the interests of a new professional class, with an emphasis on high-end services. In an extraordinary twist of history, these changes were facilitated by the political Left, using an irresistible political rhetoric of 'inclusion, diversity, access, participation and neighbourhood renewal'.[4]

Using the economics of globalisation as a means of funding, a burgeoning public sector indeed reaped rewards. Decades later, however, 'inclusion, diversity, access, participation' all remain political imperatives, but without a concrete sense of a place and space in which these can become realities. There is no sense of an active civic public in which access or participation makes sense, and no sense of a city that is formed by the people who work within it. For In Certain Places, the declining economic rationale for city life presents a unique opportunity. To excavate the history, memory and the social narratives of the municipal 'republic' style city of the industrial past, to unveil and re-present the rapidly changed demographic of the cosmopolitan multi-ethnic city of the present, and to provide a space to think about the city of the future, are all necessary stages in a process of re-conceiving the city beyond the vicissitudes of global capital. The city needs a stronger, sustainable and more resilient basis.

The city needs 're-making' in so far as the driving forces of development have been politically discredited as much as financially attenuated, and this situation will not be reversed. The situation is perplexing, where the new Localism Act (2011) and Big Society rhetoric of the current coalition government have no substantive means to implement local change, and by default are continuing an entrepreneurial agenda in the city, albeit in a weak form. Every city and every civic body is faced with the question asked by Krzysztof Nawratek in his recent book on urban revolutions: what is a city? Why is it necessary?[5] What forms of self-management, community mobilisation or other active roles can people engage in in order to re-make their city? The last two decades have been animated by a now-bankrupted optimism all propelled by large-scale capital injection. Yet there is a sense that the rhetoric of 'decline' is as deceptive as the rhetorics of the triumphalist creative city, creative class, and, more recently, smart city.[6]

As an organisation, In Certain Places emerged towards the end of the prosperous era of 'culture-led urban regeneration' (a phrase that had little substantive meaning, even when government ministers were using it).[7] For the arts, the years 1997 until 2007 were, as Sir Christopher Frayling recounted, '… a golden age'.[8] Public art agencies and consultancies abounded and thrived; many, if not most, have now closed. In Certain Places remains, and their resilience comes in part out of the fact that collaboration sits at the basis of their organisational model (with the University, City Council, city museum…), and their working practice is driven by *production*. The model of Quick and Speight is significant, as it brings together research and pedagogy, artistic practice, policy-making and the historic public institution. Through programming and commissioning, making art and managing art projects, holding seminars and workshops, generating plans, designs, and proposals, In Certain Places are identifying the political-institutional fault lines in the management of the city as well as the intellectual work required to think through the contemporary dilemma of a successful *post*-post industrial-era city. In other words, in cultural terms they are addressing the need for 're-industrialisation' as a social process, where the city re-discovers its propensity for production and self-managed change, along with its suppressed or latent capabilities for building an equitable environment.

'Industry' is often cited as the force that built cities like Preston. The distinction between 'industry' and 'economy' in political rhetoric is significant. Industry was never merely commercial, or about manufacturing, but implied a broad range of activities, from local micro-markets and suppliers, produce from the local environment, to social community, and a critical density of local skills and ingenuity. Industry emerges from social processes of 'industriousness'. Within this context, In Certain Places operate in a tension between the economics of administration and the industriousness of production. At their centre are artists, yet they function like an agency. 'Manager' and 'artist' are antithetical concepts, and ideologically central to the political contradictions of our era, defining class formations as much as demarcating conflicting value systems. Our cities have been fed a grand narrative of a 'post'-industrial era, but whose active social basis declined largely with the decline of production and the rise of administration, the decline in skills for making things and the rise in clerical skills and information-related tasks.

Yet, as Vincent Dégot pointed out, the modern manager – the central agent of the capitalist post-industrial economy – is uncannily like the artist.[9] The recent obsession for the entrepreneur in British public policy (not least cultural policy) is in part driven by the way the interpenetration of culture and economy has affected a shift in the (avant-garde) impulse from art to business. Funky Business, Karaoke Capitalism, Bobos or professional bohemians, Experience Economy, Cultural Creatives, Creative Class, all speak of the transport (or theft) of critical-cultural capabilities now recalibrated as business skills, to be seen in the new creative or cultural quarters, regenerated lofts or waterfronts, 'starchitecture'-designed luxury residential apartments in every large city.[10] As Boltanski and Chiapello state in *The New Spirit of Capitalism*, the language of corporate management in the 1990s was replete with terms like risk-taking, flexibility, polyvalency, initiative, autonomy, mobility, openness, and new possibilities, all of which were once only found in artistic culture. So then, what terms or language are left for a radical art and the artist?[11]

In Certain Places are as much about that language, and about dialogue, concepts and discussion of the city as about works of art. Their intellectual investment is not in the future of the contemporary art world, but the new discourse of artistic urbanism and the art of the city. They think about the spaces gradually vacated by the new economic class of avant-garde business, and find ways to enact a physical-aesthetic re-formation of the city through a variety of critical positions. The business and corporate world love to inhabit the spaces of prime real estate, but rarely do they possess the discursive intelligence (or ethical will) to become part of the city's *public*.

In their work, the derided brutalist Preston Bus Station roof, the old Covered Market and Market Square, empty shops, unkempt streets, Avenham and Miller Parks, festivals or celebrations, are all 're-valued' as places and spaces for defining a new public realm. In Certain Places are not politicised, didactic or polemical. They gather people in a spirit of openness, inviting them to explore aspects of the city that have been ignored, suppressed or devalued by the regimes

of commerce and economic success. The re-experiencing and re-population of devalued city spaces is a necessary step in understanding how a gathering public can 'create value', and how the inhabitants of a city can make the city a space worth investing time and energy in, out of which a profound sense of 'industriousness' can emerge. By implication, In Certain Places posit cultural production as a means by which a public consciousness of the post-capitalist city can be born, with which embryonic public policy ideas for stimulating social industriousness can be developed, and even tested.

In Certain Places, as the name suggests, attempt to find ways in which the city of Preston is made 'certain', through locating its particularity in narrative, memory, and future possibility, and in so doing the city into a specific 'place', that has a particular set of meanings and motivations for action. Yet, who understands the city? Who comprehends its forces of change, and how we engage with, or re-direct, them? Understanding corporate agencies, like property developers, is not difficult. What is difficult, is understanding the discourses of public policy, planning and the political values that drive urban development, enough to position the artist at least as interlocutor, if not agent of dissent. These powers are invested unevenly, and In Certain Places find it necessary to engage with the city's political administration, which in the last few decades has found itself with an increasing monopoly on civic decision-making, yet ever less powers in determining the fate of the city.

The urban public in Britain is subject to two dominant forces of change: the first being the aforementioned incursion by private interests into spaces once held in common; the second is an increasing claim on public goods or assets by the State. Yet few of us can define 'public goods', or where the boundary between public and private lies in the city. This is something that every city needs to negotiate for itself, but to do so we need new kinds of intermediaries and new kinds of discursive spaces.[12] The public realm, like the public, is not something static or physical but something that is convened and created, and is therefore always temporal and provisional. That makes it no less necessary and socially real.

Many public art agencies work in cities, but few take the city as a conceptual, theoretical, social and cultural problem for art, and as a context in which art is part of a spectrum of investigations requiring intellectual collaboration, research and (re-)education. Nineteenth-century Preston is a good example of how social movements, industrial innovation and public culture were, once, part of one great confluence of energy that was powerful enough to build a city. What are the forces at work constructing the city today? Generating knowledge of a once familiar place is a creative act, as public statistics, concepts of 'economy' or GDP, wealth or income, are skewed and reflect categories that are hostile to non-abstracted social, public or commonly-held wealth. In Certain Places often refer to the historical narratives of Preston, where change was wrought by politics, communities, associations and institutions, whose forms of representation, values and beliefs were explicit and openly debated. In today's city, the entire urban landscape has rapidly changed without many, if not most, of its residents or workers having any idea why or how.

A central task for a 'public' art is the making visible of the invisible forces of change, where the people of the city are able to reflect upon their role, or exclusion, in this process. The public realm is the place where knowledge of the city is formed, and a space where politically relevant dialogue can be conducted without necessary partisan interests. The last decade has witnessed impressive public art strategies from many local authorities in the UK. The roles of public art have extended from the articulation of new buildings and public walkways, to place-making and regional brand projects that reinforce local and cultural identity. It has engaged communities and supported development projects aimed at developing citizenship and participation. It is perhaps then of some surprise to find, after a decade of advanced strategy making, along with unprecedented public funding, that there is a pervasive sense of alienation, detachment, and a lack of a common project in our cities. Brands, 'smart' development, and aspirational creative city schemes can still be found in many places, but their promises ring hollow. In Certain Places demonstrate a new agenda for the city.

The new agenda for art in the city involves the activation of the space of the city for production, social empowerment through ideas, concepts and arguments for a city reclaimed by its people. The 'people' are not a homogeneous mass, for the artists invited by In Certain Places are diverse and from diverse origins. They come together, however, with a sense of commitment to the city as a project, whose history and urban space still contains a wealth of inspiration to stimulate a gathered public, without a need for global capital and unrestrained commerce. They do not just administrate or programme art projects, but are developing a deeper theoretical enterprise of knowledge creation. There are many theories of the public sphere at our disposal – showing how art appeals to the formation of counter- and subaltern publics and the multiple publics of a multicultural society. What we are short on is spatial theories of public culture, or how spaces for culture can generate the ideas, experiences and meanings needed for the social processes of 'industriousness'. Through the era of the entrepreneurial city, the term public culture came to be defined in purely financial terms (meaning 'publicly-funded' cultural activities), and where 'access' is held to be the condition of public life. This definition betrays a logic that has its roots in retailing.

This is why the art of In Certain Places is at once event, performance and participation, dialogue and research. These all come together in producing a new language of the city, and a language with specific application to the city of Preston. The experience of their art helps develop one's powers of deliberation on the shape and fate of the city, and in turn creates commonly held knowledge about that city. Possessing a substantive knowledge of a city's urban-social formation is a necessary prerequisite for the emergence of political will. This 'will' is not invested in parties or institutionalised forms of power, but in mobilisation as a self-generating, self-managed, local industriousness. As the political will of a city grows, so will its political culture. And so a new *moral* economy will emerge.

1. See B. Jessop, 'The Entrepreneurial City', in N. Jewson and S. MacGregor, eds., *Transforming Cities: contested governance and new spatial divisions*, Routledge, 1997, pp.28–41. See also S. Lash and J. Urry, *Economies of Signs and Space*, Sage, 1999, and T. Hutton, *The New Economy of the Inner City: restructuring, regeneration, dislocation in the twenty-first century metropolis*, Routledge, 2008.

2. For a classic article on this context, see D. Harvey, 'From Managerialism to Entrepreneurialism: the transformation of urban governance in late capitalism', *Geografiska Annaler*, Vol. 71, Band 1, 1989, pp.3–17.

3. See T. Edensor, D. Leslie, S. Millington, and N.M, Rantisi, eds., *Spaces of Vernacular Creativity: rethinking the cultural economy*, Routledge, 2010.

4. See the double issue of Cultural Trends, '"A Golden Age"? Reflections on New Labour's Cultural Policy and its Post-Recession Legacy', *Cultural Trends*, Vol. 20, Nos. 3–4, September–December, 2011.

5. K. Nawratek, *Holes in the Whole: introduction to urban revolutions*, Zero Books, 2010.

6. L. Kong and Justin O'Connor, eds., *Creative Economies, Creative Cities*, Springer, 2009.

7. Such as in DCMS, 'Culture at the Heart of Regeneration', Department of Culture, Media

and Sport/ Stationery Office, 2004; as a critical corrective, see M. Miles, 'Interruptions: Testing the Rhetoric of Culturally Led Urban Development', *Urban Studies*, Vol. 42, Band. 5–6, 2005, pp.889–911.

8. Quoted in S. Jeffries, 'So How Did He Do?', *The Guardian*, 2 May 2007, available online at http://www.guardian.co.uk/politics/2007/may/02/politicsandthearts.artsfundin.

9. V. Dégot, 'Portrait of the Manager as an Artist', *Dragon: The Journal of SCOS*, Vol. 2, No. 4, 1987, pp.13–50.

10. I am referring to a range of popular books, which in turn have had a major impact on public policies for cities around the world: K.A. Nordström and J. Ridderstråle, *Karaoke Capitalism: Management for mankind*, FT/Prentice Hall, 2004; K.A. Nordström and J. Ridderstråle, *Funky Business Forever: How to enjoy capitalism*, FT/Prentice Hall, 2007; D. Brooks, *Bobos in Paradise: The New Upper Class and How They Got There*, Touchstone, 2000; R. Florida, *The Rise of the Creative Class – and How it Is Transforming Leisure, Community and Everyday Life*, Basic Books, 2002; J. Pine and J. Gilmore, *The Experience Economy*, Harvard Business School Press, 1999; P.H. Ray and S.R. Anderson, *The Cultural Creatives: How 50 Million People Are Changing the World*, Harmony, 2000.

11. L. Boltanski and E. Chiapello, *The New Spirit of Capitalism*, Verso, 2005.

12. For a critical view on this, see E. Corijn, 'Urbanity as a Political Project: Towards Post-national European Cities', in L. Kong and J. O'Connor, eds., *Creative Economies, Creative Cities*, Springer, 2009, pp. 197–206.

The City and the Changing Economy
Charles Quick

Jane Jacobs has described a city as 'a settlement that consistently generates its economic growth from its own local economy.'[1]

As a group of 80 people – comprising artists, architects, local developers, planners, academics and politicians – navigated the streets of Preston, moving from one vacant property to another, sometime entering and listening to speakers, at other times hearing descriptions of why they couldn't gain access, it became evident that this was a different city from the one they had all known in 2008.

This was September 2013, five years after the start of the economic recession and two years since the announcement of the city's abandonment of the £700 million retail, leisure and residential Tithebarn plan. That scheme would have physically changed a third of the city centre, converting public spaces into productive private spaces for the retail industry. One of the advantages of the scheme collapsing is that the city retains public ownership of its markets, streets and the Bus Station. Meaning that Big Issue sellers and skateboarders can continue to populate the area without being asked to move on, and inner-city drive-in cinemas, Easter Passion performances, and other one-off events can continue to activate its public spaces.

The two-day event 'Open City Preston 2013', the latest symposium organised by In Certain Places, this time in partnership with the architects and the city council's Urban Design and Planning team, grew out of a cross-city desire to find an alternative to the failed masterplan and the perceived necessity to sell the city to developers. With the structure of the tour directed by artist Katja van Driel, artists, architects, and economists presented new processes and understandings to a range of local stakeholders. One legacy of this event has been the formation of a group of local urban design and business people, academics and city council officers, which strives to set its own agenda and influence the landscape of the city with an 'urban dentistry approach' to development.[2] One that is not about grand masterplans, erasing and replacing, but about small, incremental interventions, that maintain and reuse what's already there.

On a list of highlights following a quick audit of the city now, the following developments feature: Preston has secured the City Deal from the government, which will establish a £450 million infrastructure delivery programme and investment fund.[3] The Lancashire Enterprise Partnership – which has no mention of culture on its website but chooses to use images of well-known Lancashire public artworks from the Panopticons programme in its headers – is focusing its resources on two sites on the periphery of Preston; at Samlesbury and Warton.[4] While the investment in business and transport is valuable to the city and has been partly secured because of research by the Centre for Cities,[5] it has not stopped what the economist Paul Swinney describes as 'the hollowing out of the city centre', as the new infrastructure connected to the motorway network surrounding the city encourages growth on the periphery.[6] He also warns against trying to revive the centre through retail alone, and cites jobs and accommodation as equally, if not more, important.

Having been actively engaged with Occupy Amsterdam in October 2011, Katja van Driel and Wouter Osterholt travelled to Preston and began to map the 300 empty properties in the city centre, owned by absentee landlords, speculators, developers and the city council. In October 2012, they took up residence in an empty shop and eventually presented their findings, engaging in debate about access and ownership of the vacant premises. They highlighted the potential to use this massive resource in a creative way, to empower people to engage in a grass-roots-led change in the city rather than relying on the outside developer, which in the previous decade had been the prevailing attitude.

Since 2007, In Certain Places has used 16 different empty properties. Not to promote the sale of artefacts to the general public though. These were not spaces used for projects that could align themselves with the long history of artists using shops as alternative galleries and retail outlets, such as Claes Oldenburg's *The Store*, which opened in December 1961 in Manhattan's Lower East Side, in East Second Street, where he sold his artwork next to cheap merchandise.

These were also different endeavours than that of the artists Sarah Lucas and Tracey Emin, who set up shop on London's Brick Lane in 1992 as somewhere to hang out and sell stuff. The work from these two retail adventures now resides in the collections of MOMA and Tate Britain, and these and other initiatives could be considered as the forerunners of the pop-up shops that are now supposed to be the saviours of our city and town centres, as promoted by Mary Portas.[7]

When In Certain Places needed a base for Blast Theory's *Can You See Me Now?*, a web-based chase game, for the Internet equipment and also as a workshop space, what better place than a large shop unit in the Guild Hall Centre, central to the game and the city? As a first venture into retail spaces it set the pattern for future approaches to unearthing vacant property, often owned by Preston City Council, to be used sometimes for production, and at other times for presentations. It allowed new and varying audiences to access the debate that often surrounded the projects, as they manifested themselves in the everyday fabric of the city.

For the 2008 'Place beyond Place' symposium, Catriona Stamp guided a tour along Fishergate, the main high street in the city, and focused on a number of former bank buildings that now stood empty. Originally the local economic gatekeepers of the city, they have in recent times become part of global brands, taking control over the economic direction away from direct influence by the city. Cities have to find other ways to steer their growth and economic well-being. To facilitate this, Preston has become a Partner City in the Centre for Cities' Partner

City network.[8] The programme works closely with a small group of mid-sized UK cities, to inform economic development strategies and improve economic performance.

Other kinds of economic institutions developed from outside the area, such as Grosvenor Ltd., and Lend Lease, which formed the partnership underpinning the Tithebarn scheme, can have a negative impact on a particular area in a city. In the lead-up to grand plans, they often end up sowing uncertainty in the minds of tenants as properties are bought up ahead of demolition, commonly known as 'planning blight'. Often this process is seen by local authorities as a necessary evil that will be offset by the bright promised new future. Ahead of the Tithebarn scheme, the St. John's shopping centre – then owned by Grosvenor – began to empty out, leaving its remaining tenants, some of which are still there, concerned about the diminishing footfall. One of In Certain Places' propositions was to invite artists Teresa and Dominique Hodgson-Holt, Martin Hamblen and Leo Fitzmaurice to temporarily inhabit three of the spaces, which they used to explore what alternative uses could be given to retail property. Their approach was to suggest another kind of retail that was based on experiences that circumvented the economics of the high street. In the Shops Now (2009) was a local creative response to a situation orchestrated by outside global influences on the city.

A view of Preston that encompassed the range of local with the national/global merchandise was Local Colour by Becky Shaw, who, over three months in the summer of 2008, photographed all the clothes in the windows of fashion shops along the main retail streets of Preston. This process connected twelve independent retailers whose shops became outlets for the free prints that demonstrated the local colour of Preston and the 'subtle differences of place'.[9] Since then many of the local retailers have gone, swept away in the recession, and even some of the national chains have been replaced by franchises of even bigger chains. Guy Rubins predicted this when he spoke in Preston (in 2006) about the relationship between (local) businesses moving out and being replaced by the narrow economic models of the (international) chain store, homogenising the appearance of every high street, and the negative effect this would have on the specific sense of an individual place.[10]

It is interesting that some people quantify the stature of a place by the range of high street chain stores it hosts. What new visitors would John Lewis, whose flagship store would have been a key element of the proposed Tithebarn scheme, have attracted to Preston? Cities simply do not wholly rely on retail as their major economic driver; services, manufacturing, and people taking up residence are part of this complex dynamic too. Although Richard Florida's writings on the so-called 'creative class' verbalised a prevalent interpretation of the processes of inner-city regeneration and development, which has in recent years been heavily critiqued, there is a long history of artists and communities realising new possibilities of use for vacant buildings of any size.[11] A number of public buildings that surround Preston's Flag Market, and that help give it its sense of grandeur, are now entirely or partly empty. Does a city abandon these properties as they decay, hoping for a knight in shining armour on a white horse to come to the rescue (cue developer), and hand over what is public to become private? Or does it look to the community of artists, creatives and entrepreneurs of the city to populate theses spaces and so help generate growth from its own local resources? Whereas some ten years ago, the preferred recipe would most definitely have been the former, In Certain Places' activities have hopefully contributed to a more nuanced approach and opened the door to maybe less grand visions for the future, but ones in which initiatives can evolve that are already embedded in the city's tissue, like Rebecca Chesney's weeds.[12] Something that Jane Jacobs would approve of.

1. Jane Jacobs, *The Economy of Cities*, Random House, 1969, p.262.

2. John Thorp's analogy for carefully working on separate elements of the urban landscape without damaging the neighbouring parts. 'Open City Preston' presentation, 2013.

3. Notes from Cabinet, 8 July 2013. Report of the Chief Executive Lancashire County Council.

4. Lancashire's Panopticons are a unique series of twenty-first-century landmarks, designed to attract visitors into the countryside to enjoy the stunning landscapes and wealth of attractions that this area has to offer. Each Panopticon is situated on a high-point site commanding spectacular views.

5. The Centre for Cities found that Preston had the third highest growth of private-sector jobs out of all of England's cities in the decade prior to the recession (1998 to 2008).

6. 'Supporting Economic Growth in Preston', December 2011, Paul Swinney and Zach Wilcox, an independent report by the Centre for Cities.

7. 'The Portas Review' is an independent review into our high streets, conducted by retail guru Marty Portas.

8. Preston is not a member of the UK's eight core cities like Manchester, Liverpool, and Leeds, but is recognised as one of 26 mid-sized cities and is taking the lead in working together with other cities.

9. Artist Becky Shaw talking about the project.

10. Guy Rubins from The New Economics Foundation spoke in Preston as part of 'Talks and Debates' on 26 April 2006. His talk was titled 'Ghost Towns, Clone Towns and Home Towns'.

11. Richard Florida, *The Rise of the Creative Class – and How it Is Transforming Work, Leisure, Community and Everyday Life*, Basic Books, 2002.

12. See Rebecca Chesney's *Tanpopo Tour*.

Becky Shaw, *Local Colour,*
Preston High Street/Fishergate

'The relationship between supply and demand fascinates me. What comes first, the climate that produces the desire for a certain colour, or the decision by the industry to create it? And how do we understand the relationship between local identity and global industry? While all Topshops are pretty much the same, why, for example, does the window display on The Strand, London, feel more "calypso" than the store in Preston?'

Becky Shaw, 2008

Local Colour is an artwork created by Becky Shaw after visiting Preston's high street and noticing differences between the clothing ranges on offer in Preston and those in other UK cities. Over the summer months of June, July and August 2008, Shaw photographed every item of women's clothing on display in all of Preston's shop windows. These photographs were then arranged to form a series of charts, which mapped the 'local colour' of Preston's high street and mirrored the changing colours, textures and patterns as spring/summer moved into autumn/winter. The charts were reproduced as a set of three special limited-edition art prints, which were distributed by the staff of independent fashion shops in Preston, by placing them in customers' carrier bags every time they made a sale. The project concluded with a performance lecture by the artist, hosted at the University of Central Lancashire.

June–November 2008

In the Shops Now!,
St. John's shopping centre

'In the Shops Now!' was a month-long residency, during which artists developed projects in three recently vacated shops, in a semi-open-air shopping centre. During the residency, each artist worked in a specific shop, instigating collective performances and developing installations, which were displayed for a further month.

Teresa and Dominique Hodgson-Holt,
Red

As part of 'In the Shops Now!', Teresa and Dominique Hodgson-Holt created an alternative shop, where customers took part in a unique performance by temporarily exchanging their clothes for red outfits and taking a walk through Preston city centre. The project cumulated in a *Red* flash mob on Saturday 1 August, during which 30 people, dressed entirely in red, walked through the city's streets, squares and shopping centres. Following their residency, Teresa and Dominique developed the project in Bury, Greater Manchester, where they took over a stall at The World Famous Bury Market.

July–August 2009

for your
comfort
and safety

do not touch
smoke panels

no push
chairs

hold young
children

Leo Fitzmaurice, *Archigraph*

For 'In the Shops Now!' Leo Fitzmaurice transformed the frontage of one of the centre's externally-facing shops into a modern-day stained glass window, which was illuminated at night.

July–August 2009

Martin Hamblen, *Heuristic*

During his residency, Martin Hamblen worked from 9am
to 5pm, Monday to Friday, constructing a 'tunnel', which ran
through the middle of his shop, and creating a series of films
and interactive installations. Shoppers were invited to chat
with the artist, or leave him messages, which informed his
subsequent activities in the space.

July–August 2009

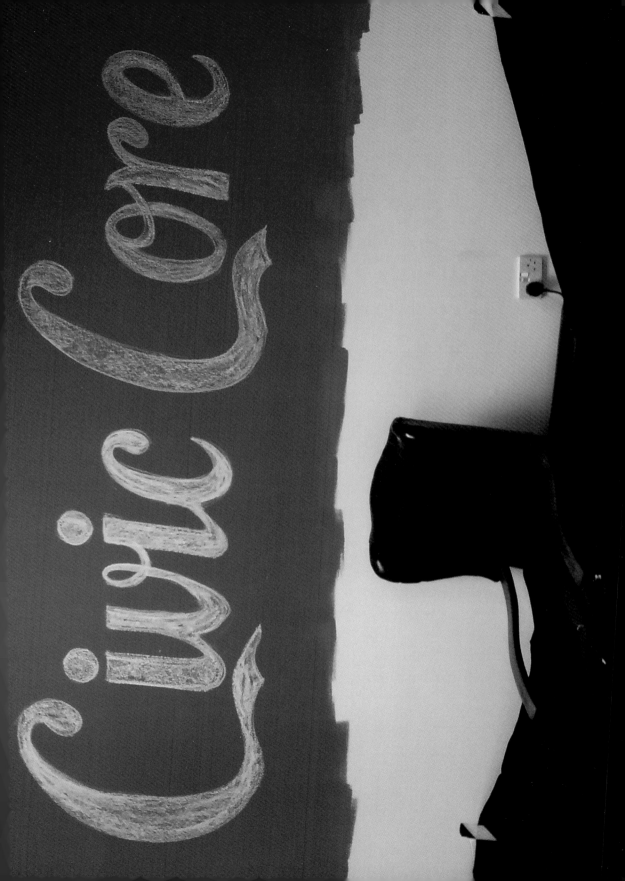

Martin Hamblen

The good thing about In Certain Places is, generally speaking, the openness to let the artist do what they want, which to me seems the most appropriate way of working. From a selfish point of view that's the way Fine Art should be. If you are given too specific a brief it stops being Fine Art. It becomes something that's prescribed, or it becomes art as social work. You're doing something to tick a box, which, somewhere back along the chain of command, is being ticked because of funding or something like that. Whereas, if you are just told 'work away', 'crack on, it's all good', that's the ideal scenario. It becomes more like graphic design when you're given a brief.

Even if initially people don't like it, if it provokes them to start thinking about something, then that ultimately is a good thing. The thing I like about durational performance is that as people go about their everyday life, they clock you, they notice you. Then it takes it outside of the tick box. The fact that you're there regularly gives other people more opportunity to be curious. That's why I do the nine to five, 40-hour week. I had lots of conversations with people and it's something that you can't quantify, it's all qualitative information that I, as the artist who's there all the time, pick up on. People will say 'what is it?' I'm not going to give them an answer, but the start of the conversation is 'well, what do you think it is?' Having a conversation is better than just looking at something and then reading a text about it. People can be dismissive, but at the same time they can be surprised.

Provoking a conversation is positive; the opposite would be that people are numb to their surroundings, or oblivious, or accept how things are.

Katja van Driel and Wouter Osterholt, *Open to the Public,* Guild Hall shopping arcade

'The struggle for space is an important political conflict, which exposes power relations. Empty spaces provide an opportunity to talk about ideas for the city, as well as to open up places, which can be shaped by different communities to produce a new type of "urban commons".'

Wouter Osterholt and Katja van Driel, 2013

Open to the Public was an action research project by German and Dutch artists Katja van Driel and Wouter Osterholt, which explored the potential of empty buildings to create new types of access to the city. During autumn 2012, the artists spent time mapping the many underused and vacant properties in Preston city centre. The following January, they invited members of the public to view their findings, which were presented in an empty shop unit in the Guild Hall shopping arcade, and to share their own opinions and ideas about the future of the city. The artists also hosted public discussions with community activists and local authority officers, including Preston City Council's Head of Property Management, about the causes, effects and possible uses of Preston's empty buildings.

October 2012 and January 2013

OPEN TO THE PUBLIC

Open City

'Open City' was a two-day programme of talks, debates and workshops, which examined the current condition of Preston city centre and the various plans and aspirations for its future. The event, supported by North Lancashire Society of Architects and RIBA North West, employed Preston as a case study for exploring the contemporary role of 'mid-sized' cities in the UK, and presented creative responses to urban development.

The event included presentations by architect John Thorp, economist John Swinney, and artists Jen Southern and Jeanne van Heeswijk. In addition to the university, the talks took place in an empty church, a disused art institute, and an abandoned council office. Participants were also led on a walking tour of other vacant properties in the city, curated by Katja van Driel. During the tour, actor Abigail Ramsdale read out a series of conversations between van Driel and the owners and gatekeepers of properties to which she had attempted to gain access. Presented inside or in front of the buildings, these dialogues provided an insight into some of the barriers that prevent the productive use of empty spaces in the city.

During a day-long workshop, participants were encouraged to share their own experiences and ideas about Preston, led by artists Charles Quick and Gisele Bone, architect Ann Vanner and human geographer Hannah Neate. This included mapping exercises, which revealed different perspectives of Preston, and led to a number of proposed cultural activities, such as community cinemas and artists' studios, which could help reanimate disused areas. The discussions and ideas signified a move towards a more flexible approach, built on consensus, partnerships and debate.

September 2013

Open City

It was around 2009–2010 when my involvement with In Certain Places began. I was a volunteer assistant for the symposium 'Place beyond Place'. What I always like about the symposiums is the mix of speakers – there might be an architect, an artist, or an urbanist. I really enjoyed it, because you can get such a range of experiences when you volunteer with arts organisations. Some will stick you on your own for ten hours, just doing nothing and not speaking to anyone, while others provide a good experience. So fortunately this was at the latter end of the scale. From there, I kept up with what you were up to and volunteered for every symposium since.

I also worked on the project *Open to the Public*. We spent quite a lot of the time with the artists, who were looking at empty properties. We spent a couple of days meeting with them, talking with them about their ideas. We also took trips around Preston, finding empty buildings and taping them up with fake crime scene tape, which was fun.

In 2012 we did the 'Open City' event. As a volunteer, that role was probably the most challenging. It involved a tour around the city, where the venues popped up along the way. So it was our job to arrive ahead of everyone else, quickly set up chairs, set up projectors, so that when everyone else walked in it was all ready. That was quite fun, but a real challenge. It was fantastic to be in all those buildings – places that I've walked past every day for a couple of years and thought, 'oh God what's in there?'

It's always a little bit different. It's different venues, unusual spaces, there's a mix of speakers that you wouldn't normally get. There's always an opportunity to talk to these people and get different points of view that you wouldn't otherwise have an opportunity to hear. The second day of the 'Open City' event was more of a workshop, with a lot of architects and city planners, for example. We were with them all day, getting to chat with them and see how they see the city, how it functions for them, and how they contribute to it. I think that's been really valuable to me. I've been here six years and you think you know it, that you know these streets. But you can still be shown something totally new about somewhere that might be five minutes from your doorstep. It's not just the mix of people, but the mix of locations is also important. The journeys around the city keep you on your toes – you do look for different signs and different things around the city. Whether it's in Preston or elsewhere, those things stay with you and you look for the CCTV spots, or the funny little alleys, or the edges of a town.

There's a unique mix of people at these events. A lot of them, for example city councillors and other people with the power to make decisions in the city, are people you should be able to have some access to, but often they stay in their offices. So it's nice to have them in a room all day where you can ask them questions about things that you want to know. I also think it's politically interesting to expose those people to a lot of arty types. During 'Open City' I spent quite a long time talking to a city planner. He was showing us how he would navigate the city and how he would plan it or how he'd write about it, how he'd approach it. So when I went back to my own work, it gave me a new approach. It's quite refreshing as a practice – it gives you a whole range of different starting points. Or similarly, the economist was very interesting. He had these different maps, based on wealth, or commerce, or things like that. So again, it gives you this whole range of different starting points that you wouldn't normally think of if you just carried on down the usual route that you take in your practice.

How In Certain Places operate and the quirky interests that it has fit well with what I'm interested in. Even just having these new contacts is quite useful. It's great for me to have those different kinds of connections that I would probably struggle to make on my own.

> Steph Fletcher,
> Artist and volunteer

One of my passions is supporting Preston and its branding, helping to give character to the city. Having worked on this Guild for four years I have focused all my energy on promoting arts and culture, as well as inviting participation, the key to getting people on board.

The knowledge I gained at the 'Open City' event was more in the benefit of analysing the movement of people in order to host events in the best place. The people who attended the conference really cared, and the events I've been involved with over the last few years have placed me with people who want to make a difference. They and a coterie of Guilders are heaving with ideas. The Guild binds some people in a definitive way for Preston. There is creativity to be harnessed.

How do the people in Preston station orient themselves, find a light bite, a proper meal? We need to pose the questions and provide the answers... I think if the Guilders had an hour or two with one of your team more ideas would come.

> Brenda Dell, Preston Guild
> volunteer and 'Open City'
> participant

My perceptions of the issues that Preston faces haven't changed, but they have shifted. From feeling 'unable' as an individual to do much, I feel a greater sense of empowerment due to the collective nature of the event and the understanding that others had similar feelings. The hope came from the fact that Preston City Council was represented, and the empowerment from the range of individuals who are clearly interested in the contemporary urban environment.

> Ann Vanner, Architecture
> Lecturer, UCLan, and workshop
> leader for 'Open City'

The Vacancy Walk script
Katja van Driel

Owner: Baptist Union Corporation Fishergate Baptist Church
Where: in front of the church

Step 1: Email invitation to real estate agent Peter Townley of Longdon & Cook

Step 2: Email answer by Steve Wing, Baptist Union Corporation:

Your email to Peter Townley of Longdon & Cooke has been passed to us as we are the property owners and he is acting as our agent in the disposal of the chapel building.

Regrettably whilst we can see benefits to being part of the programme of events that you are putting together there are internal problems with the building which would mean that the likely insurance costs to us to open the building to the public in the way you have suggested mean that we cannot be part of it. Added to this the local issues of opening up the building and the distance we are from Preston as we are based in Didcot Oxfordshire mean that unfortunately it will not be possible to include the building as you have highlighted.

I am sorry that we have had to decline your request but hope that the programme you are planning is well attended and successful.
With kind regard

Steve Wing, Deputy Manager, Baptist Union Corporation Limited

Step 3: Answer by email

Dear Steve,
Thank you for your answer.
We understand that you do not want to be troubled with further cost regarding the building. Therefore we want to offer you to cover the insurance costs incurring for this event.

What we can also offer you is broad public attention and profound discussion regarding your building. We want to offer access to structures that are, at least temporarily, lost for public or communal use. We do not only want to talk about possibilities, but also create them — even if it is only on a symbolical level for the moment.

We would be very pleased if you could agree to discuss the finding of ways to make it possible to get inside this building.

Step 4: Second reaction by email from Steve Wing

Thank you for your follow up email.

I am sorry but even though you have offered to cover the insurance costs incurring for the event it will still not be possible to use the building as part of the floor has been removed to deal with wet rot and a new floor has not yet been installed. In addition there is currently no electric that can be used in the building as they need to be completely renewed and upgraded which we will not be carrying out prior to the sale of the chapel. Because of this due to Health & Safety concerns I regret that we do need to exclude the interior of the building from the event.

Step 5: Contact the local Baptist community, phone call to Richard Spalding

Step 6: Email to Richard Spalding

Hi Richard,

I will attach the invitation for the event. We want to organize a tour along vacant buildings to let the participants see what is already there on the ground and to uncover why those buildings are out of use, what that means for the inhabitants of the city and also to try and open as many of them as possible for a viewing.

Step 7: Answer by email from Richard Spalding:

The church is owned by the Baptist Union of Great Britain, and I believe you have been in contact with Steve Wing, their representative.

He is concerned about Insurance for your guests, and Health and Safety and unwilling to let them in.

Can you tell me if your conference carries insurance that protects your guests when visiting buildings?

Can you re-assure us that your guests are in supervised groups, so we can keep them away from unsafe areas? (we can have representatives available in the building to guide them too) Meanwhile I have arranged for details of the activities held at the church before it closed to be sent to you by Alan Edward, who attended the church.

Regards
Richard

Step 8: Email answer by Richard Spalding

I have now got agreement for you to enter the Fishergate church building PROVIDED I can get insurance. Please note that I will be in attendance, and that they will need to comply with my instructions. Also, you can explore the ground floor, but the basement floor is unstable, and people will only be able to look into that room, and not enter it.

Step 9: Email answer by Richard Spalding

I have confirmed that the Insurance would cover persons from injury caused by faults in the building but it is necessary for you to confirm that your event has Public Liability Insurance for injury / damage caused by your delegates during the function.

IF YOU CAN CONFIRM THAT YOUR EVENT HAS PUBLIC LIABILITY INSURANCE, WE CAN PROCEED.

Entering the building: reading the 2nd part out loud
Where: inside the building, while people are taking seats

Email answer received
by Alan Edwards

The Fishergate Baptist Church building
has been used in a number of ways
since 1991:

1. Most obviously it was used as a
   place of worship on Sundays and
   other days by the resident Baptist
   fellowship which numbered about
   20 people at the time of the close
   – these people now worship at
   various places nearer to their
   homes – none were from Central
   Preston. It was also used as a
   place of worship by the Preston
   Chinese Gospel Fellowship.

2. The foyer was regularly used as a
   'coffee shop' serving drinks and
   biscuits during the day on certain
   days of the week in exchange
   for donations – no fixed charges
   were set.

3. The foyer was also used for
   a regular 'homeless' persons'
   drop-in each Monday evening,
   attracting 20+ people each
   time – soup and sandwiches
   were available and food was
   distributed as well as donated
   clothing and bedding

4. The basement was used regularly
   by a dance school on Fridays.

5. The basement was used on
   Wednesdays as a holistic support
   centre for homeless under-25s.

6. The University used the basement
   regularly as an examination hall.

7. The basement area was used also
   for prayer meetings.

8. The basement was used for
   social events by most of the
   church users from time to time.

9. As well as the building being
   listed the organ has an Historic
   Organ Certificate Grade II
   'being a good organ by Henry
   Ainscough c1875 substantially
   in original condition'.

The building closed on 31 August
2010 for regular services due to
the high cost of maintenance of
the building and the lack of funds
available to do so. Being a listed
building any materials used in
building works are required to
be 'as original' which makes
it an expensive proposition. The
building was severely damaged
by an IRA bomb in 1991 and the
cost of reinstatement was not
supported by the Government so
all the funds had to come from
Insurance and Donations in that
year. Then, in the period 1992 to
2012 some £70,000 was spent
just to maintain the building.

Since 2004 significant effort has
been made to find a solution
for the long term survival of the
building including use for social
housing at the rear, adding a
floor to maximise use of the
space, introducing office/retail
space etc. Plans were drawn up
and much effort made to explore
possible solutions. However, the
funds to effect such proposals
were not available and attempts
to find grants were not successful.
In the end it was agreed that
the building should close before
further costs bankrupted it –
each local Baptist church is
responsible for its own costs.

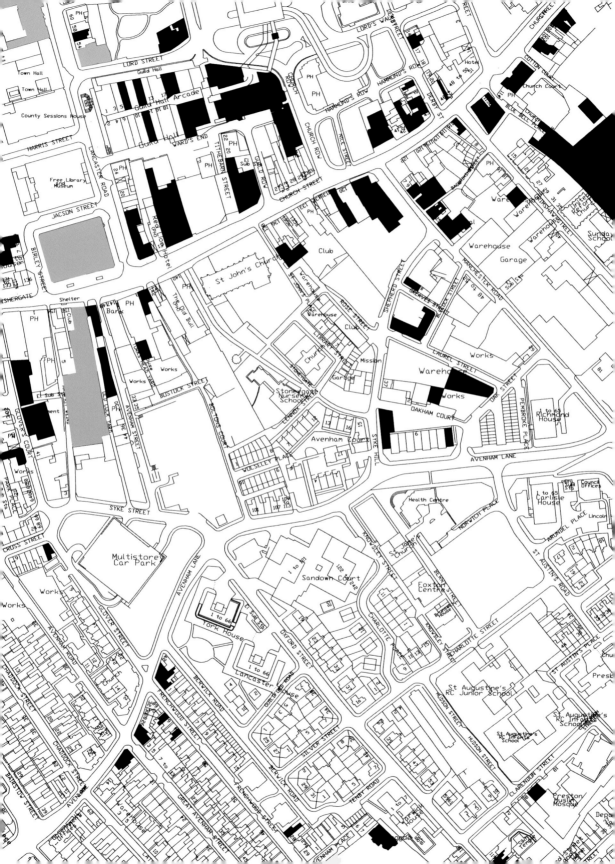

Katja van Driel

After so much research and walking around the city, it is hard to remember what my first impression was. One of the clues I have is to look back at my photos from the first walk, and a lot have danger signs on them. You are very much watched over in the city, and there are a lot of regulations that restrict your movements in public space. This has been one important common thread throughout the project. When you follow discussions around what is called 'austerity politics', the question arises: can we afford all these regulations in the current climate, and are they even desirable? The price of avoiding risk is high, and not only in terms of public expenditure. By implementing so many regulations you avoid direct contact between people, meaning that negotiations always require institutional mediation. Within these circumstances, it is hard to understand what one's personal responsibilities are, and it is, of course, not conducive to experimentation.

You get a direct sense of the consequences when walking around the streets of Preston: a particular type of space for unexpected exchange and informal encounter is missing. Coming from the outside, it was not easy to figure out where to go to meet people who would wish to get involved in a discussion. So the project, in the very first instance, was about exploring strategies for 'space making'. The empty buildings in the city centre became a vehicle for thinking about the possibility of protecting non-defined spaces, while at the same time demonstrating the ways in which the current logic has failed. During our time in Preston, we met a lot of people who shared with us their perspectives, and came across different initiatives that were not so immediately visible. So, looking at the built environment from a certain perspective also helped us to locate the social relations in the city. *The Vacancy Walk*, during the 'Open City' symposium, focused on this in a more direct way. Of course, it was about negotiating space, but it was also about revealing and untying existing power relations in the city. I think this is a necessary step when you are interested in creating spaces for the future.

A certain fixation with the past was another thing I noticed when I first came to Preston. People seem to be very nostalgic, which is a provocative thing for me. I am interested in finding ways to deal with the past without nostalgia, which see it as a vital part of the present situation.

The collaboration was very open. It gave us a lot of space to explore, to learn more about the place, and to experiment with different ideas and approaches. You [In Certain Places] were really generous in that and the result is that this was certainly not a project imported from a different place or context, but developed in a dialogue with the location. What was challenging, at times, was the fact that we found very little infrastructure. It often took some time to organise things, but you always had a way to resolve it. This is also how we gained an understanding of what it takes to run an initiative like In Certain Places in a place like Preston: there is always some pioneering involved. This is also partly why we ended up imitating the structures of an institution. We somehow had to invent a structure within which to communicate. What I am curious about is your expectations when inviting foreign artists, and how far your expectations are met and what you take from that experience.

Revisiting Utopia

'Revisiting Utopia' was a symposium that brought together architects, artists, urban planners and people with an interest in the future of cities, to examine the role of architecture in an age of austerity. Employing Preston's iconic Bus Station as a case study, the event explored the modernist principles that informed the construction of the building and discussed the architectural impact of recent urban regeneration schemes, such as the planned redevelopment of Preston city centre that threatened to demolish it. Examining issues of environmental sustainability and the significance of local knowledge, the event asked to what extent the utopian ideals of modernism, and the buildings they inspired, might still be relevant within today's urban landscape.

The symposium featured talks by architecture writer and journalist Owen Hatherley, and architect and author Irena Bauman, and a panel debate, which was chaired by Lancashire County Councillor Kevin Ellard, and included Preston City Councillor Tom Burns and Christina Malathouni, Senior Conservation Adviser at the Twentieth Century Society. The day also involved a bus ride and tour of the Bus Station, and an exhibition of artworks inspired by the building, curated by artist Steph Fletcher.

Preston Bus Station was designed by Keith Ingham of Building Design Partnership, and is an example of brutalist architecture. Completed in 1969, it has 80 bus bays and is the largest bus station in the UK. It includes a multi-storey car park, and is linked to other parts of the city via subways and an elevated walkway. Threatened with demolition for over ten years, it was finally granted Grade II listed heritage status in September 2013.

July 2012

Revisiting Utopia

The idea that modernist buildings are utopian shows just how far we have moved to the right.

Owen Hatherley

The recession has offered space to re-imagine how our cities could work and to focus on the small, not iconic.

Irena Bauman

The council have become property developers rather than city planners.

Audience member

The growth agenda in recent years has been directed at cleansing our city centres of the poor.

Irena Bauman

Would it be possible for a community group to take ownership of the Bus Station, as it provokes so much passion?

Audience member

The Bus Station is outstanding. It works and it's a wonderful piece of urban design.

Irena Bauman

The city should be about something else than shopping. We need to find a new perspective.

Tom Burns,
Preston City Council

We need confidence, vision and quality for Preston.

Kevin Ellard, Lancashire County Council

You Need to Understand What the Priorities Are

A conversation between Lubaina Himid, Charles Quick and Elaine Speight

CQ What was your motivation for starting to work with In Certain Places?

LH I suppose I got very cross because you seemed to be doing what I often have an issue with; working with an artist from somewhere else and bringing that artist to Preston. When I have been the artist from somewhere else, I want to know about the artists who are there. How do they cope with this institution, or where do they buy cerulean blue, or what kind of studios do they work in? If I'm going to be in a place, I want to know what kind of place it is. How does it function? And I investigate that through the people who are there.

So I was worried that In Certain Places would be a project in which people, artists, would come here and imagine that nothing happens. That there were no artists, that there was no culture; that it was just a dump. There were some interesting conversations happening, and I wanted those conversations to be heard by the artists who came here. I could see that it could be a bridge between what culturally was happening in Preston already, and the way in which artists from somewhere else can sometimes see things that can't be seen by the people who actually live here.

CQ How did you arrive at choosing the artists you wanted to work with from Preston?

LH I suppose for years, for decades, I always wanted to work mostly with women artists, with black artists, because it's still really challenging in a kind of ludicrous, old-fashioned way for artists who are women, or artists who are black and women, to actually negotiate a conversation. Either with the world of art in public places, or the world of museums, or, shall we say, the hierarchies that allow or enable a city or big institution to function. I have always tried to be the kind of person who puts their foot in the door, and then tried to allow other people to come in with me. So I wanted to work with those people, because I wanted to know what these artists think of this place, or this situation, or this project, or this life, or this shopping centre, or this queue that we're in, or this invisible place that we sometimes inhabit in a city. I wanted to see if those conversations could be had with other women, or to a slightly lesser extent other black people, who live in this city.

There are not many, but that in itself is kind of interesting in a region that has large cities like Liverpool and Manchester, where a very particular apartheid system functions in terms of where black people go and where they don't go – in terms of shops, events or whatever. In Preston many of the black people who live here, certainly at the beginning of In Certain Places, were people whose families had lived here for a long time. Now many more black people who live here are African students who have come quite recently. So in that time all sorts of things have shifted, but in the beginning I was trying to make more public the kind of conversations I was having.

ES   So it was about visibility?

LH   Yes, absolutely. I'm mostly concerned with visibility. The notion of belonging is another reason why the project really interested me.

ES   Last time we talked, we also discussed the issues of asking, and the difficulty that some artists have in knowing who to ask, or which questions to ask, in order to access opportunities in the city or to gain that visibility.

LH   Yes. Until In Certain Places happened, it didn't occur to me that you could actually have conversations with a city. It would never occur to me to ask a city a question, or expect it to follow any other agenda but its own.

I'm not particularly good at asking. What I do quite a lot is do something and then assume that it will be alright to do that thing. But I would never ask permission to do the thing, because I would assume that whoever it was would say 'no', and would find a perfectly good reason.

As In Certain Places developed, I could see that there were faceless people that In Certain Places made human and had real conversations, real meetings with, real negotiations about the place, the politics, the economics. And that you perhaps ask bigger questions than some of those people had ever asked themselves. I thought that was a really interesting way of working and something was revealed.

ES   That took a long time: moving from the asking to having a dialogue.

LH   You didn't ask Joe Bloggs from Manchester, you asked Alfredo Jaar. He came along, you did those presentations. You invited faceless beings from the council. They came. You asked and they came. And that was early on.

CQ   Yes, that was because we understood how to ask, and because it was a partnership between the university and city council.

LH You were asking from day one. So it might have taken a long time to get any kind of answers, but it's always been about presenting the possibility of partnership, the possibility of collaboration.

CQ It took a long time before we had any sense of impact, before we had a sense that they were listening to us.

ES But that's about two things: the first is about trust and spending all those years building relationships with people in the council, and the other is a lack of other possibilities in today's economic climate.

CQ That's absolutely true, and it isn't just here but everywhere. It's undoubtedly changed the way people look at cities and how they work, for the better.

You've obviously worked with many arts organisations right across the world, and you're often the artist who goes to other places, as you mentioned earlier. What sort of distinctive approaches do you identify with In Certain Places.

LH That genuine freedom for the artist to do whatever they want to do. Other organisations may say that's what they're doing, but

I do genuinely believe that you are actually interested in what those artists do in this place. And that you allow them to do it, and you enable them to do it, because you could allow them until you're blue in the face, but if you didn't enable them as well then it wouldn't work.

It's completely the opposite to me making work in places that want desperately to stay the same, and so only allow a negotiation or a dialogue if I promise that everything will stay the same. Of course, that isn't my intention, but I do always promise: that I won't break the pots, I won't scratch the mahogany tables, that it will be absolutely fine. I'm always negotiating with people who are absolutely particular about keeping things the same. I love the way In Certain Places says, 'here's the city, we'll show you every inch of what we know of it and then you tell us how we can enable you to do something.'

My observations of some of the artists that I've worked with with you, is that you set the bar very high in terms of artists using their initiative and being able to carry the project. So I sometimes found myself having conversations thinking 'well that would be interesting if it was a bit more of a triangular conversation', and acting as a conduit between In Certain Places and the artist, rather than working as a temporary partner on a particular project. It still works for the artist, usually, that way of talking to me, where I'm saying, 'well that bit of it you're going to *have* to go and ask Elaine, or you're going to *have* to get Charles to help you do that, because I don't know how to negotiate it. You're going to have to go back to them'.

So that's probably the most difficult bit of it. But the best bit is seeing those artists being able to stand back from the work and realise that they have, with your help, set up something that's bigger than they thought it could ever be. They've surprised themselves with what they've done. I think that's what really works for me about the project: it allows artists to understand how effective they can be.

ES   That's something that we've learnt from talking to you, because at the beginning I think we expected artists to ask us all the time about everything, so we didn't really ask to be asked.

CQ   Because we are asking people aren't we? We ask.

ES   We see ourselves as that broker between the people who can give the permission for these things to happen, or help them to happen, and the artist. But you're right; perhaps sometimes that wasn't clear for the artists we were working with.

CQ   Another interesting thing you were saying was about how we facilitate the work, and how we're also gatekeepers. When

we bring artists to Preston, we begin by showing them the city, but it's through our own eyes, because it can only be that to us. So we are framing Preston when we show it to people. Some people sidestep that and go and find a different Preston. But we are gatekeepers as well, because we provide the access, which enables them to do what they want to do.

There's a lot of, I wouldn't go as far as to say collaboration, but partnership. And the nature of the practice means there's a lot of dialogue and negotiation. We could say to an artist 'you might really want to put the work there, but you might have to put up with having it here. Are you going to be able to put up with having it here?' And then there's lots of discussion about what that might mean for the project. So we do have a very subtle impact in that sense, simply because the nature of the practice means it generates a lot of discussion about all aspects of the work.

ES   There's a lot of negotiation. It is very different creating something in a space in a city instead of in a white cube gallery. Maybe some of the difficulties that have occurred when we've been working with artists who haven't worked in that

way before, are because
we take for granted that
that negotiation is going to
happen and that's a big part
of the work.

Q   Yes, or it's taken them
aback a bit, because they
have a particular view
and I suppose for this type
of practice that's only the
starting point for the work.
The thing then travels
quite a long way before
you get to the end. But the
advantage of that, which is
what you're talking about,
is that you can end up
with something far greater
than you started with. And
that's because of all these
conversations you have along
the way, which bring in
all these other things, and
connect the work to all sorts
of situations, so that it
can grow.

LH   Yes, but you do seem to have
two different ways of working
with artists. You work differently
with Shezad Dawood and John
Newling than you do with
Chantal Oakes and Susan Walsh.

CQ   Yes, absolutely.

LH   But when you say 'we work with
artists in such and such a way',
you don't always make that
distinction between the two,
because you're using one set of
artists to say one thing to and
with the city, and another set
of artists to say another thing
to and with the city. The man
in the street doesn't know the
difference between John Newling

and Chantal Oakes, but you
make a distinction; you make
a decision about which is more
able to have the dialogue with
the city. There is a different
way of working, a different way
of funding, a different way of
following up, a different way
of presenting the work later; a
different relationship with thos
artists. And I don't think that
matters, but when you use the
word 'artists' and you're giving
talks in public places, you just
talk about artists. But you have
particular hierarchies of artists
and completely different ways
of relating to them: you choose
artists for their experience of
working in the world of art, ov
artists with less experience of
working in that world. It isn't
really to do with public space
or not, it's to do with being
able to negotiate big art projec
or not.

I think you're following the
market and you're following
the art world system more tha
you've come to terms with.
I don't think that you shouldn
I just find that you follow
exactly the same system as the
gallery curators, but you don't
quite admit that.

It's obvious to do that because
it's much easier to get money,
it's easier to talk to those artis
because they have an experien
of negotiation overall: negotiat
their time, negotiating money,
negotiating an idea. But who's
to say that somebody who
intimately understands the cit
but doesn't have a practice as
established as Shezad Dawood

or Becky Shaw's couldn't make a project that shifted conversations much more effectively than those artists who came in and went out, who are in effect negotiating their own careers via In Certain Places? Loads of really good things have happened, but I think that you missed a trick. Not that you stopped doing it, in that there *are* artists who understand the city intimately, who might not be that glamorous and not that well connected, but who, with the same amount of enabling, negotiating, funding, follow up, could have made shifts that we can only dream about.

The point about the city is that it is fantastically complicated. And you couldn't know how complicated it is, which of course sometimes stops you doing things; the more you know about it the less you can do about it. But it's so complicated that I've come to admire artists who really want to know things very deeply and to know a place very deeply.

It's a different kind of discussion that I've had before about flying into a place, doing a project and flying out. This is kind of, 'what would it be like if these people really, really interrogated this place, and the far reaches of this place?' There are fringes of it that In Certain Places doesn't quite reach.

CQ   No, we haven't attempted to reach them.

LH   And strangely that's where the people are. In the centre, here, are the transient people:

university lecturers who live somewhere else, or the council officers who live somewhere else, or the shop workers who live somewhere else than the place where they work. So in a way, the projects do interrogate the city, but they don't interrogate necessarily what makes up the city, which are these people on the fringes, some of whom don't even ever leak into the centre.

CQ   We did one project, *The Family* on the Brookfield Estate. But there are other transient populations that live in the city as well. There are the students, and then there's the different immigrant groups that live in the inner city, the poor inner-city areas that you have in lots of cities, but in Preston on a much more reduced scale. Those people engage in the city centre, they sometimes shop in the city centre.

LH   They do, but if you live in Avenham or Frenchwood, you see the people who live there. If you go to the corner shop you might pass 30 or 40 people who are on their way to the mosque or the corner shop. But then, if you go to Marks & Spencer or even the market, you're never going to see even one of those people.

CQ   Yes, not even in the market. We noticed that with John Newling's project.

LH   Because the market is an absolute bastion of white working-class life, and long may it survive, but there is an apartheid still going on. It is just a little bit leakier here than in other places. The university is not an apartheid place; it leaks in one direction out from the centre, and the communities that live in the inner city leak out a bit. But there's this place with the grand and fantastic architecture of the city, where you would think you were in 1970s Preston; it's exactly the same.

CQ   Our focus has always been on the city centre, simply because of the history of the project, growing out of a response to Tithebarn. Obviously it's grown past that now. We're aware of that bigger city. We've just got to work out ways to engage with that, because at the moment we engage with the city centre, where, as you always say, you can walk everywhere within ten minutes. That's the sort of city we engage with – we understand the logistics and how it works. But if we start to engage with a city where you need to get on the bus or navigate by car, then that's a different type of experience, and we've got to get our heads around that.

LH   But the ten minutes from St. John's Minster to the prison, that's a hell of a ten minutes; it's another country. The ten minutes from the prison to the football ground is another country. But that's not even the leaky edges, I'd say that was still the city centre and still

within those ten minutes. And then the ten minutes from the football ground to the university is another odd corridor. But that's without Ribbleton, which is another country again. Geographically and historically it's strange.

CQ   I remember you saying – and it contradicts a little bit what you've said today – that we don't really engage in the art world, in terms of the gallery art world. And that we've enabled some of the artists we've worked with to leapfrog some of those hierarchies that you get in the North West, in terms of galleries. In the past you would show on the staircase first at the Harris, and then you'd show at the Turnpike, and then you'd have a group show at the Bluecoat [Liverpool]. But we don't engage with that.

LH   You eschew all that because you know it's a waste of time, so you are engaging with artists at a higher level, with artists who were in danger of going on that same route. I've said to some artists, 'look, I'll get you to work with In Certain Places because they can make things happen.' So absolutely, indeed you put more money into some of those artists' projects than they'd ever had put in before, especially without filling in a 27-million-page form.

So that was a huge leapfrog, but behind the scenes there was an awful lot of follow up and an almost day by day, going backwards and forwards with detail, that didn't happen with In Certain Places. So then, when that situation is a bit more confident and a bit more ordered and sorted, some of those artists feel safer, better, more confident to come back to you, to then start asking the next sort of questions.

ES For a long time it was a case of 'boom, boom, boom', just delivering things all the time, without a space to have these kind of curatorial discussions with artists, either during or at the end of the projects. That's something that we've been thinking about quite a bit lately. The 'Practising Place' programme is perhaps one way of having certain types of conversations with artists that aren't about negotiating with the city, but about the important things within their practice – their motivations or their ideas – and trying to have these conversations publicly, in a way which involves other people.

LH There was some point, early on, when we worked together, where I thought that I could make a book. I believe in the book, as a different project than the artworks, as a place to have some of those sorts of conversations. Giving yourself time to reflect on what you've done is important. Because your projects are always about something being there and then not being there; the evidence of it, the discussions

about it, are gone in the ether. So doing this book is really welcome.

CQ You're giving us too much credence in terms of having thought about every little bit. It's a journey in that sense. So, one thing leads into another and you readjust this and readjust that. We're not working in the same way as when we first started, because the project has changed from its early days and the aspirations have changed. All along it's kept changing, which has been its strength really. It's been a case of being reflective and thinking 'OK, well that didn't work, let's try and do this'. All our funding is for two years or one year, so the project has to change continuously.

ES Yes, but all the decisions we make are conscious ones.

CQ Yes, we're widely tactical.

ES Exactly. For example, the thinking around working with some of the more established artists from other places was tactical; although we absolutely wanted to work with them, they also had a kind of currency. In order to access certain funds we had to be seen to be working with artists who were operating at a particular level. That's why a lot of the artists we worked with share similarities in terms of their backgrounds and where they are in their careers.

LH I'm not saying for a minute that those artists weren't interesting: they shifted things incredibly. It did work. The thinking around the city has changed. The Covered Market is different having had the ghost of John Newling in it. It changed. So all those were brilliant decisions. But, in terms of working with you, it's never been very clear where things begin and end – what the artist's role is, what they're supposed to be doing, and how much leeway they've got. I would always say to those artists 'well, you know, Charles moves with the deadline, if the deadline shifts, that doesn't faze him.'

CQ Yes, I think our motto is 'it's got to be at the right time'.

LH But that's such a privileged position. People are 45 and they're dying sooner than they should do. So, 'it's got to be at the right time' is a Nick Serota phrase. With the privilege of being able to see 500 years back and knowing that his career will arch in a particular way, he will always say that these moves will only be made at the right time.

CQ I don't think we see it in that global way. It's more about whether it matters if it happens this month, or if it would be better two months hence.

ES That decision depends on the weather for example.

CQ The weather is important, and audience is important, as are all those other things that happen in a city.

ES It goes back to the fact that we're working in the city and not in a gallery, and that we often have to negotiate when things happen.

CQ We don't have as much control as you might like to think we do, and we're working in partnership with lots of organisations, negotiating permissions and funding. It's no accident that Shezad Dawood's *Piercing Brightness* premiered during the Preston Guild. That was worth quite a lot of money to us and for the project. So yes, there are always lots of different things pulling and pushing in different directions.

LH Yes, I've thought about this a lot, as you can imagine, and I don't think I'm as critical of it as I have been. I just think it's a way of working that's completely different to the way in which I work. Part of that is because I work with museums, and I work with them because it's easier to see a tangible change than in the city, and because, quite a lot of the time, it's easier to get to the people that make the decisions, even if you can't actually change their minds.

In this city, where I've lived for 23 years, I feel completely powerless and completely voiceless and invisible, even though I live in a very grand house in a very lovely street overlooking the park. There aren't actually any lines of communication. So if you're a householder, even in a lovely street, you can't have any say over what happens to that street.

ES   Because we're trying to think about how we develop the project, we were interested in what you think the priorities should be for our work and what we should focus on.

LH   That is a really good question. Why are you doing it? There could be a number of reasons, couldn't there? It doesn't seem to be about empowering people, which is a bit of an old 1970s phrase. So if it isn't about that, what's it about? This morning, Charles was talking about an article that he'd read in *Public Art Review*, which wasn't talking about what In Certain Places did, but about the sorts of things that In Certain Places has achieved, or has attempted, or the questions that In Certain Places has asked. And I think that you have to work out how to get yourselves seen as the model for this way of working. Because I've been talking for years about In Certain Places as the best model for talking about how artists can influence a changing city.

If I were to set up a parallel project to In Certain Places, it would have to be a kind of guerrilla organisation – In Other Places, or something. What

interests me are those hidden places: the church round the back of Winckley Square, or St. Wilfred's, which is hidden in plain sight. It's a metaphor for how I see political situations. In those two cases it's a set of people making a particular kind of contribution to a city, but hidden, disguised. So I would only be interested in having guerrilla and underground conversations, where you probably could never prove anything. What I'm trying to understand is, if the place you were talking about were in France, for example, what would you be looking at? Is Preston just the place we all landed in from outer space? Or is it the perfect model because it's got one of everything? Or is it actually so peculiar that you could have made even more effective and visible shifts than you maybe think you have, if you had done this in Wigan? Because Preston is strange, can it actually not be done here, whatever it is; because it's destined, in a peculiar way, to be the way it is, resistant to change and steeped in its own complicated history?

It's not quite clear whether it goes: 'us as curators, artists, Preston, the people of Preston'; or 'the people of Preston, Preston the city, us, In Certain Places'. You need to understand utterly what the priorities are. But then I would say that you have to nurture your artists as if you were running the most wonderful London gallery. They have to have a sense of belonging to you, because they'll do more work than you could ever do alone.

That's what Magda is doing in Vienna; even though you had to put an awful lot of work in to get her there, she's working for In Certain Places. Susan is working for In Certain Places in Durham and working for In Certain Places when she's making those plaques, because she never would have done it without already having done *To Scatter.* She did that because she understood the city, and she understood the city because she'd been part of In Certain Places.

So lots of these artists are working for you, but they don't have a sense of belonging to you that you've engendered. And you could do that. You could get that for free and they could do lots of the work for you. So some of the time that means identifying where you need to follow things up, and where the artists are contributing to your project. I talk about In Certain Places all the time. So *I'm* working for you. Even when I'm most cross with you, I would talk about In Certain Places.

Lubaina Himid MBE is an artist and Professor of Contemporary Art in the School of Art, Design and Performance at UCLan. In 2004, Charles Quick and James Green invited her to curate a programme of temporary public artworks by Lancashire-based female artists, as part of the In Certain Places programme. These became *Beside the Seaside...* by Pam Holmes (2006), *Remote Viewing* by Patricia Walsh (2006), *Thoughts That Make Actions in the World* by Chantal Oakes (2008), *The Arcade* by Magda Stawarska-Beavan (2010), and *To Scatter* by Susan Walsh (2010). Lubaina has also acted as a mentor to many of the early-career artists that In Certain Places has worked with, and has been an important critical friend from the beginning.

The best projects I have worked on have grown out of conversations, which have been allowed to happen through more informal relationships, after you have got past the 'Dear Sir or Madam' formal introductory emails. It's better to just pick up the phone or send a text or have a pint in a pub. I think that's the point at which people become more honest and open, and I suppose In Certain Places helps people to relax and become that way. I have always felt as if I have been able to speak honestly and openly with you. You are very transparent about what you are doing. The enthusiasm about the city and what you are trying to do comes through and that's what people latch on to.

The most interesting or exciting things that I have worked on weren't predetermined. They have been about learning to trust artists, and knowing that they will find where the interesting things are. They will certainly challenge you; as an organisation they will force you to think differently, you'll work harder in certain areas, certainly. Often it's much more fruitful for both sides if the people you are asking to respond are given the freedom to do that fully, and in their own space and time. We are very keen to think about how artists are given the right level of support, and that's a very difficult thing to determine because we work with local and emerging artists right the way through to established artists. Clearly there are different needs there. You came first by starting the conversation, but I think that we now do that too.

Richard Smith,
Curator, LICA
(Lancaster Institute for the Contemporary Arts)

Senses of a City
Elaine Speight

When an artist, or indeed any In Certain Places associate, visits Preston for the first time, we take them on a walking tour of the city. If it is a sunny day, we might meander through the magnificent Avenham and Miller Parks, breathing in the earthy aroma of the tidal River Ribble as it ambles towards the sea, or put our ears to a manhole cover in a residential street, listening for the subterranean River Syke. In the more common event of rain, the Covered Markets provide shelter and the opportunity to unearth rare vinyl records or haggle over some musty-smelling curio. Regardless of the weather, we will always pick out landmarks from the Bus Station's blustery top deck, and return to the city centre via its echoing subways or walkways in the sky. If time allows, we like to reflect on the day's events over a pint of local beer, among the Victorian tiles and Brasso scent of the city's Black Horse pub.

Like many artists and curators who create projects in and about a place, these first-hand experiences of the city form the basis of our practice. This tactile approach is also what sets In Certain Places apart from official attempts to inform the future of the city. Urban regeneration, in particular, is a process of visualisation. It begins with data – facts and figures about the economic and social demographic of a location, which are used to form the graphs, pie charts and reports that present the case for regeneration. This is followed by a cartographic phase, where the topography of a site is mapped to locate opportunities for redevelopment, and boundaries are drawn and redrawn. Next, a visualisation of the city, post-regeneration, is projected through scale models, architects' impressions and marketing slogans, designed to sell the scheme as an idealised, yet achievable, future. Therefore, if and when the regeneration is finally achieved, it constitutes, above all, the fulfilment of a vision. Yet, while this process may provide useful information about the physical or economic aspects of a site, it says little about how somewhere feels, or the significance that it holds for the people who move through it. Artists, on the other hand, deal primarily with meaning, and are thus well placed to locate the important, yet often overlooked, specificities of a place.

The human geographer Yi-Fu Tuan distinguishes the concept of place from that of 'undifferentiated space' by describing it as 'consecration of value'.[1] Unlike the spaces that urban development seeks to erase and transform, places are profound centres of meaning, which are produced through the memories, emotions and values that people attribute to them. As such, the lived reality of an environment can often be very different to external perceptions of it. In Chantal Oakes's abstract animation *Thoughts That Make Actions in the World* (2008), the bold, confident lines of Preston's Bus Station are juxtaposed by modest marks that the artist found scratched into the original wooden backrests. Praised for its monumental stature, sculpted curves and photogenic qualities, the Bus Station has become a cause célèbre for enthusiasts of modernist architecture. However, for Oakes, the graffiti scratches signify attempts to convey a sense of humanity within an otherwise colourless, draughty and inhospitable space. The artwork, therefore, tells a story of the Bus Station as a lived and practised place, rather than simply an object for the architectural gaze.

Urban planners have long acknowledged the need to physically interact with the site of their practice in order to understand it. Inspired by the 'on the ground' approach of urbanists such as Jane Jacobs, they spend considerable amounts of time walking the avenues, roads, streets, paths and desire-lines of their cities. A similar sensibility can also be found in the practices of many of the artists that we have worked with. John Newling began *The Preston Market Mystery Project* by manning a stall in the Covered Markets during an icy week in November. Setting up and dismantling his stand each day, alongside his fellow traders, the artist gained an intimate knowledge of the rhythms and relationships of the market by becoming part of, what geographer David Seamon describes as the 'place ballet' of the site.[2] Likewise, Lisa Wigham's textual intervention *The Waiting Room* (2012), was informed by her explorations of Preston's hidden and quiet locations, and her observation that the city more readily reveals itself when encountered at a leisurely pace.

The geographer Paul Rodaway describes how the two interpretations of sense, in terms of *making sense* through 'order and understanding', and as a 'sensation or feeling' experienced through the body, are 'closely related and often implied by each other'.[3] Embodied engagement therefore provides a useful strategy for understanding the physical, emotional and social workings of the city. Artists, however, are not simply the receivers, but also the creators of meaning, and the artworks produced through In Certain Places have encouraged people to sense the city in new and surprising ways. Magda Stawarska-Beavan and Collaborative Space, for example, provoked new readings of the Harris Museum & Art Gallery by imbuing it with the soundscapes of Kraków and Florence respectively, while Patricia Walsh's sound piece *Remote Viewing* (2006) disrupted the ambience of cafes and shopping centres with accounts of the supernatural. Jeppe Hein's interactive water sculpture, *Appearing Rooms* (2006), meanwhile, transformed Preston's underused market square into a performative social space.

As well as revealing and engendering meanings, the non-visual senses also play valuable roles in the social life of a city. As part of our talks and debates programme, cultural sociologist Monica Degen described how, during the regeneration of Barcelona's notorious Raval area, the removal of balconies effectively destroyed the neighbourhood's sense of community. By isolating the smells and sounds of everyday life within individual apartments, the redevelopment abolished the sensory bonds that existed between the inhabitants, resulting in feelings of segregation and quiet, soulless streets. In contrast, by reconnecting people to the city in shared and sensory ways, artworks have the ability to create new forms of sociability. David Henckel's collaboration with a local craft brewer, for example, produced a new Preston taste and tradition. Named after the astrological event that occurred in 2012, The Transit of Venus ale will be brewed in Preston once every 20 years. Created as a contribution to the Guild, the artwork facilities and celebrates the shared encounters that inform senses of a place.

It is predominantly through our bodies and the sensory tools that they possess that we perceive and connect with a place. As an instrument of orientation, measurement, mobility and coherence, the body 'mediates between us and the environment, giving us access to a world beyond'.[4] In Certain Places, then, could be thought of as a corporeal project, through which the meanings of a city are perceived and communicated in the form of shared encounters. As conduits of experience, the artworks produced through the programme have provoked new sensations of place, which have encouraged the city's residents, visitors and decision-makers alike to re-evaluate their existing perceptions. By engaging with the lived realities of Preston, in all its complex forms, the artworks eschew notions that a city can be quantified or known. Instead, they persuade us to immerse ourselves within it, and present new possibilities to touch and be touched by the place.

1. Yi-Fu Tuan, *Space and Place: The Perspective of Experience*, University of Minnesota Press, 1977, p.6, p.12.

2. David Seamon, 'Body-Subject, Time-Space Routines, and Place-Ballets', in Anne Buttimer and David Seamon, eds., *The Human Experience of Space and Place*, St. Martin's Press, 1980, pp.148–65.

3. Paul Rodaway, *Sensuous Geographies: Body, Sense and Place,* Routledge, 1994, p.5.

4. Rodaway, op. cit., p.31.

Chantal Oakes, *Thoughts That Make Actions in the World,* St. John's shopping centre

Thoughts That Make Actions in the World is an abstract animation, which was created in response to Preston Bus Station, a unique 1960s building which is said to be the second largest in Western Europe. In 2008, the building was earmarked for demolition as part of Preston's Tithebarn regeneration scheme. Chantal Oakes created the work in response to her observations of the site – specifically the graffiti-covered backrests that line the bus bays. Rather than the subjects of mindless defacement, the artist viewed the backrests as objects 'annotated with marks brought about as a by-product of powerful thoughts'.

The resulting animation constituted a regeneration of these exclamations, coupled with the artist's own visual statements of engagement with the site. The work was projected onto the windows of a disused shop unit in the St. John's shopping centre as a three-screen installation. The animation was timed to denote the paced appearances of people and transport, and the flow of air, heat, echo and noise, and thoughts while waiting in line.

February 2008

Chantal Oakes

The Bus Station is a landmark. It has a lot of history and there are a lot of people in Preston who worked to build it. But I wanted to look at it because I had no relationship with it at all. I never went there. So when I got this commission with In Certain Places, which was about regeneration, I thought I'd have another look. It's very difficult to catch a bus to go out to the suburbs, and it's not a particularly pleasant place. So I really wanted to have a look at it, to see how I could describe what it's like to be in the Bus Station. I was working with abstract moving image, and I wanted to see how that could be placed in an environment that had big blank walls, without colour and movement in it. How would that work? There were things that interested me – particularly the scratches on the back of the backrests, they are the only porous surface in the Bus Station.

My work was about the place and the 'play' of the place. The light, the light on the tiles. The wind, the noise of the wind. The voices, the very few voices. The frustration, you know, scraping into the back of the seats late at night. You can just image people sat there, completely frustrated with both the wait and the place, and the lack of humanness in it. I still have no opinion on its architectural value. I have no idea if it has value or not. As a space, as a container of air it's quite interesting to just go round and be childish about it. Hopscotch around! That's all I was interested in, my own reaction to it.

I wasn't going there to glorify it. I wouldn't use it, it's slippery and cold, I don't think it works well against the setting it's in. There's no colour, no movement, nothing that catches the eye. It's a very sterile environment. So there were a lot of things going on about how negative I thought the site was.

If there's one thing I love in the place, it's the benches. The ones that are quarter curved. They're really nice, even though there are now some metal chairs dumped in with them. I just hate the white tiles, I don't really like those! Even those curves that go out, they're so counter-intuitive. If you stand anywhere near them it's almost like they're going to take you out and over. I like how huge it is, imagine if that was a playground – that would be fantastic! It's very much a playground with the rubber flooring, like an indoor playground. There were lots of things that influenced the abstract images that I came up with.

The project raised all the issues about where an abstract animation goes. Is it just so obscure that it can only exist in a university, or an art gallery? If you place a human being in front of it, does that work? I think it actually does. I ended up making a piece in the Maritime Museum in Liverpool. Using the idea of a person between the film and the audience worked really well.

Eventually I found something interesting called concrete art, which was developed about the same time as brutalist architecture. It didn't mean

concrete in the sense that it's made
out of concrete. It meant that line
and colour are enough, concrete in
themselves, to make an image, or to
make something that's absorbing and
which people can watch.

What drove me onto the next stage
of my practice was thinking about
how you can relate and respond to the
work if you don't know what it's about.
Rather than reading it as a flat surface,
how do you get into the thing? Maybe
because I made it, I could see into it,
but I don't know if other people could.
I thought there was a real issue with
that. One of the first animations that
I did afterwards was designed for a
dancer to move alongside it. So that
was the next idea.

David Henckel, *The Transit of Venus*

The Transit of Venus was a collaborative project that took its inspiration from the rare astronomical event when the planet Venus passes across the face of the sun. This event was first observed and recorded in the Lancashire village of Much Hoole by Jeremiah Horrocks in 1639. In 1927, an observatory was built in Moor Park, Preston, which was named after the Liverpool-born astronomer, and in 2012, the Transit coincided with the Preston Guild for the first time in history.

The artwork, which reflected on the temporal relationship between the two events, began as a collaboration with Arkwrights, a small craft brewing company based in Preston, to create a real ale to celebrate the Transit. It developed organically through tasting events in the brewery and at Much Hoole, where members of the public recorded their observations on the beer's appearance, flavour and aroma. The final ale was a strong, hoppy, pale 7.1% traditional English IPA. The project culminated in a tasting event on Winckley Square, as part of the Preston Guild celebrations, and a craft brewing competition at The Continental pub in Preston, where independent brewers submitted beers to sit alongside The Transit. By imposing the Guild's aesthetics of celebration upon the Transit of Venus event, the artwork considered how local traditions can be instigated. Following the 2012 Guild, The Transit recipe was filed away, and the artist plans to submit it to the Harris Museum's collection. The next time the ale will be brewed will be to celebrate the 2022 Preston Guild.

September 2012

John Newling, *The Preston Market Mystery Project*, Covered Markets

The Preston Market Mystery Project was developed through a series of visits that John Newling made to Preston during 2005 and 2006, in which he became intrigued with the city's historic Covered Markets. The artist was particularly interested in the activity of transaction and exchange that defines the markets, both with respect to the transaction of goods, and the social exchange between the people who work and shop in the space. The project was developed to celebrate this exchange and to begin conversations about importance of the 'unknown' within a city, how mystery contributes to a sense of place and what this means in the context of regeneration. The project consisted of three separate but interrelated events: *The Insurance Stall*, *Voicing Mysteries* and *The Knowledge Meal*.

For *The Insurance Stall* (November 2006) the artist hired a stall in the Covered Market, from which he 'sold' specially designed certificates insuring against 'loss of mystery' in return for shoppers' stories of mystery in their lives. Over a three-day period he collected 280 mysteries, which included stories of lost objects, haunted houses and even possessed mobile phones.

During a twilight performance, in March 2007, Newling stood in the middle of the larger Covered Market and read each mystery aloud from a golden lectern. Of the 280 collected, the artist selected the 30 most mysterious mysteries. The people who had submitted these stories were invited to a three-course *Knowledge Meal* in the larger Covered Market in June 2007. As well as bringing market users together, the event also provided an unusual spectacle for people passing by, many of whom stopped to listen to the guests' conversations, which were amplified in the space.

The Knowledge Meal guests were reunited the following summer, as Newling invited all contributors to watch a film about the project in the Covered Market. During the event, everyone who had submitted a mystery was gifted a copy of a limited edition of *The Preston Market Mystery Project* publication. This contains all 280 stories, alongside visual analysis of the mysteries, and the mystery of mysteries, number 281: 'Why is it that more women than men refer to lost items, dead people, places and houses in their mysteries whilst more men than women refer to animals, questions, and travel in their mysteries?'

The Preston Market Mystery Project provoked a re-evaluation of the Covered Markets as spaces for evening performances and events. This led to other activities in the space, most notably a drive-in cinema, which was organised by Preston organisation They Eat Culture, Preston Guild and Abandon Normal Devices, as part of the AND Festival in 2011.

November 2006–June 2008

he mystery of the market place

ists are being drafted into the redevelopment of Preston, Lancashire. **Richard Holledge** finds out why

Speaker's corner: conceptual artist **John Newling, right, is one of the artists hoping to add inspiration to the redevelopment of the city which boasts the Harris Museum, left**

work of a conceptual artist can be a ...nely. So it is for John Newling, who is ...d in front of a lectern which glows ... the gathering dusk, reading an ...ently random selection of statements. ... audience in the Market Place, ...n, compromises one man munching ... of chips and a brace of ...graphers. A couple wander by ...g puzzled. Yet Newling plods on with ...g ... the 280 Mysteries he has ...ted even though the market is empty, ...stacked, its pretty Victorian ...ation highlighted by erratic lighting. ... work is called Voicing Mysteries and ...es a collection of utterances from the ... of Preston about their unexplained, ... and wonderful moments. "Twenty ...ars ago I separated from wife," ... one person's story. "I lost touch ...y daughter. One letter with no ... address - 'I'm OK will see you soon'. ...s 10 years old at the time. Five years ...got another letter - 'things aren't ...right', that was last I heard." Why he ...ard nothing since then is left ...lained. Newling moves swiftly on to ...t question: "How many buttercups ...t bees on them?"

...he real mystery is, what's this got to ... the redevelopment Preston, Lancs? ...an example of artists getting involved ... future of a city. Preston council has ...ced a £500 million deal with ...nor Estates to transform the ...arn area of the city centre by 2013, ...t the sixties' high rises, knock down ...station and replace the 1.6 million ...feet with 400 new homes, ...ants and a hotel, not to mention a ...en cinema and *mirabile dictu* a John ...tore.

neo-classical Harris Museum looms magnificently over a cobbled square and a fine open market. There are some heroic statistics: it boasts the deepest single dry dock in Europe, the doomed bus station with 80 bays is the biggest of its kind and it had the country's first by-pass. It used to be the Bath of the North, a centre for lawyers and accountants, but what it needs now is some imaginative architecture, a touch of poetry.

Charles Quick, an artist and teacher at the University of Central Lancashire is a man with a mission to make sure that what happens next to the city will not be botched as it was 40 years ago.

He says: "Last summer we commissioned the artist Jeppe Hein to create an installation for the market. He gave us Appearing Rooms in which the 'rooms' consisted of walls of water, appearing and disappearing randomly, letting people walk from room to room.

"It made people look and think again about the way the city could be. We have teamed up with the Chilean artist Alfredo Jaar because we believe it is essential to get artists involved in the development

plans. The city is keen to have us ... the council and the North West Development Agency is behind u... gives us the opportunity to get in ... the planning process."

The council agrees. A spokesma... "It's not just a shopping mall. Wha... looking for here are new streets a... city centre. Using public art has al... been part of the project."

The original draft for the develo... was drawn up by renowned archit... Farrell in 2002 and has since been ... modified, but the influence of Alfr... as the 'exterior eye' to Quick's loca... perspective will be fascinating.

Quick says: "He gave a talk to 15... city's main players about spaces an... opportunities. They were thinking ... differently and seeing things again...

"This is the man who was comm... to work in a town in Sweden. Every... was funded by the paper factory – ... houses, the church, the leisure cen...

"Jaar noticed there was no muse... he made one out of paper and pers... artists to contribute. The opening ... packed. The project lasted 24 hour... he burnt the place down.

"Such were the protests from the ... residents that the paper firm has ag... build a new museum.

"The lesson for us here is obviou... cannot wait for the development to ... sorted out without us so as well as ... involved in talks and organizing de... we are staging public and tempora...

Which is where John Newling co... "My kind of event gives another co... the place I am in and encourages pe... see things differently, even for the ... time. Artists are very good at an ov... if dyslexic about the detail. They c...

HE MADE A

help guide the artist along. It's given me confidence in the process and about stripping back the information and presenting a more reduced text. It's helped me to understand my approach – presenting a very brief piece of text as opposed to telling the whole story, and people do respond quite well to that. It's about believing that people will do that as well, because of the responses that I've had back from the piece in the train station. I've had curators approach me independently of any other connection saying that they wanted to talk about this piece.

Patricia Walsh, *Remote Viewing*, Brew Cafe, Equator Cafe, Guild Hall shopping arcade

Patricia Walsh was one of the first artists to be commissioned by In Certain Places. Her artwork, *Remote Viewing*, is a seven-minute soundscape, which was played in various venues across the city centre over a two-week period in summer 2006.

The title, *Remote Viewing*, refers to the psychic phenomena of extra-sensory perception (ESP). The sound piece includes an instrumental passage called 'Eternally' by the jazz bandleader Cyril Stapleton, and a series of extracts from conversations that explore ethereal beings and environments. Played twice a day in cafes and a shopping centre, the artwork caught people unawares, drawing them into an intriguing audio experience, and shifting perceptions of time and place.

June 2006

REMOTE VIEWING
(07:25)

PATRICIA WALSH 2006

patricia.walsh6@btopenworld.com

Remote Viewing
(07:25)
Patricia Walsh
CD 2006

Bringing Preston to the World
Sophie Hope

'Perhaps we could imagine space as a simultaneity of stories-so-far.'

Doreen Massey[1]

Sometimes, the architecture and people of cities are supposed to act as romantic, neutral backdrops in front of which the artist-as-flâneur acts out their fantasies. This is not the approach of In Certain Places. I want to focus here on two of their projects to see how they offer spatial montages of 'stories-so-far' of a complex, ever-changing city. The text is interlaced with quotes relating to some of the ideas and questions arising from my thinking about the city, art and change. They act as resting points and temporary distractions throughout, rather than explanations or external evidence. I have primarily engaged with the documents relating to *Supervised* by Laurence Payot (2012) and *Local Colour* by Becky Shaw (2008). This has allowed me to think through the idea of Preston as a 1:1 scale stage set that the artists are observing, capturing and editing, allowing fact and fiction to mingle. While writing this, the streets, squares, monuments, markets and shopping centres of Preston have become life-size replicas of a contemporary retail city, with characters moving through and props and scenery filling it.

'There are nearly thirteen million people in the world. None of those people is an extra. They're all the leads of their own stories. They have to be given their due.'

Cadan Cotard in *Synecdoche, New York*[2]

The work of In Certain Places is not intended to redesign the city, but to shed new light on its changing state and reveal something about its social fabric. In commenting on how artists develop ideas, Preston resident Pam Moores, in Chris Davis's project *The Family*, suggests 'it's like doing a jigsaw' (2008). Fragments and traces of ideas, images, observations and encounters build up to create multiple, contrasting pictures. This can be seen in the work of Shaw and Payot, who both collaged 'data' collated from their research of the city. These two projects create unsentimental re-workings of the awkward clutter of daily life and polished, fetishised versions of urban dwelling. But before I explore these two projects further, I first want to introduce a piece of public art in Preston that was funded and supported by the Preston Trades Union Council, Preston Labour History Group, Preston Borough Council, Lancashire County Council, the Art Department of Preston Polytechnic (now UCLan) and North West Arts in 1992. This sculpture tells a binary story of Preston in which the 'goodies' and 'baddies' are carved in stone. The two projects I will then look at introduce less oppositional narratives, but still draw attention to the invisible powers and injustices at work in a twenty-first-century city.

> 'The contemporary public domain is the place where we are meant to meet each other, where the staging of the encounter is more important than the question of whether the encounter is motivated by democratic or purely commercial interests.'

Jeroen Boomgaard[3]

On 13 August 1992 a sculpture by Gordon Young was erected on Lune Street to commemorate it was 150 years since soldiers opened fire and killed four cotton-mill workers. They were taking part in a demonstration of over 3,000 striking workers demanding better wages in the mills in and around Preston. Strikes were happening across the country in the summer of 1842, in response to the rejection of the People's Charter by the House of Commons in May that year. The Charter demanded decent rates of pay, better working conditions, and fairer political representation for the working classes. The sculpture depicts a line of four chunky soldiers, shoulder to shoulder, hats pulled firmly down, pointing rifles at three figures, one covering her eyes, one his crotch, while the other has his arms bent back over his head. The huge workers are kneeling before the soldiers as if surrendering to them. This harrowing confrontation is mounted on a stone platform, low enough to step onto and walk between the firing squad and their targets, the defeated demonstrators. The memorial aims to act as a permanent reminder of the sacrifices working-class people made in trying to improve working conditions and democratic processes. With 50 per cent of all children living in Preston apparently being part of families suffering from the financial depression since 2008, this struggle continues well into the twenty-first century.[4]

> '"Your task isn't to create the sculpture," he said; "it's to strip all the other stuff away, get rid of it. The surplus matter"...
> Now, I wondered how to find my building... What I needed to do was ease it out, chisel it loose from the streets and the buildings all around it.'

Tom McCarthy[5]

On 11 May 2012, artist Laurence Payot took digital photographs from the steps of the Harris Museum of Market Square from 8am until 5pm. She then manipulated the images to create a new set of documents that tell a different story of the square. Six categories of people are singled out and appear in six different images. In one, the square is empty apart from 7 people in mobility scooters or wheelchairs traversing the space. In another, 20 white men are captured walking alone, and in another 23 couples walk arm in arm. In the next image 17 cyclists are peddling in different directions and in another 26 people are loaded down with shopping bags. In the final image we see 25 people wearing hijabs and taqiyahs walking through the square. Payot states:

> 'The categorising technique I used is very similar to the one used in monitoring forms, where we become a tick in a box, but transforming it into a visual form makes it look strangely humorous, as well as ironically dark and sectarian.'

The Cenotaph in the background of each image is a memorial to the beginning of World War I, and Payot's project formed part of the process of renovation of the Cenotaph to mark its centenary in 2014. The slice of Preston life these images captured in May 2012 show an open civic space being traversed by different characters, mostly in the act of moving from stage left or right to get to the other side. Although the images are still, I get the sense people are moving across the space rather than stopping to reflect on the war or the civic-ness of it all.

> 'The number of our doubles is infinite in time and space. One cannot in good conscience demand anything more. These doubles exist in flesh and bone – indeed, in trousers and jacket, in crinoline and chignon. They are by no means phantoms; they are the present eternalized. Here, nonetheless, lies a great drawback: there is no progress... The universe repeats itself endlessly and paws the ground in place. In infinity, eternity performs – imperturbably – the same routines.'

Louis-Auguste Blanqui[6]

According to *Trend Fashion & Forecasting*, this summer (2013) women are supposed to be wearing clothes that reflect the

> 'craft tradition of Africa, Marrakesh's vibrant mosaics and patterns, the simplicity of ceramic crafts, go garden [sic] with the beautiful fruit and vegetable prints often found in quilting, intricate lace patterns, vintage from many different

periods in the 20th century and shine and luminosity.'[7]

This is a change from 2008's forecast, which predicted a summer of whites, bold prints, the return of flower power, hot ethnic accents ('think India, China, Indonesia and South America') and apparently green was going to be browner.[8] I have no idea if these vague conjectures actually came to light, but artist Becky Shaw decided to carry out her own survey for her In Certain Places commission. Fascinated by the relationship between supply and demand, the local and global and why Topshop on London's Strand felt more 'calypso' than a store in Preston, Shaw took a photo once a month in June, July and August of 2008 of every women's clothes shop window in Preston. She then went through the labour-intensive process of cutting up sections of the images to create three colour charts for Preston, each representing the 'local colour' of June, July and August 2008. The charts were then printed as three limited-edition posters and distributed to shoppers of selected independent shops. In her performance lecture that marked the end of the project, Shaw presented a slide show of the original images she took of the shop windows while talking about the process, using the three months as chapters in her story.

> 'The city is a space of not only substantial but fleeting discourse: what tools are at our disposal for tapping into and exploring this chatter?'

Greg Smith[9]

A city's colour is diagnosed using thousands of images of limp clothes hanging off Preston's mannequins.

The demographics of a civic square are captured, dissected and distilled to present six visual charts. For both projects, photographing the same locations over a sustained amount of time is a repetitive exercise, each click of the camera capturing any changes that might have taken place. At the same time, there are more seemingly static, fixed elements – some of the fashions haven't changed, the Cenotaph is still there (although even that has changed with its renovation). These city spaces are observed, documented and then that information is edited and presented back as collages of the traces of consumers, protestors and pedestrians at particular times and in specific spaces. Reducing the complex and contradictory nuances of society into a colour chart or simplistic demography mirrors the commercial practices of the city. The six images in *Supervised* could have been used by the companies photographed by Shaw as market research for potential target groups of consumers. Each individual crossing the square is reduced by Payot into one visual characteristic, such as (dis)ability, religion, marital status. Their personal views and experiences of the city remain a mystery (we have to listen even harder to the stone carving to hear what stories the long-dead cotton-mill workers have to tell). Is it enough to assume their stories must be diverse and multiple? The colours assembled from changing shop window displays by Shaw provide a palette informed by global trend predictors and Preston's window dressers – how 'local' is the colour and does it matter? These are partial extracts of an infinite number of other configurations of colours, pedestrians and struggles that make up strata of narratives that might merge together or miss each other, happily complicating the idea that a city might have its own identity. What these extracts offer up is the question of what (and who) is left out in the stories of uncertain places.

'A space exists when one takes into consideration vectors of direction, velocities, and time variables. Thus space is composed of intersections of mobile elements. It is in a sense actuated by the ensemble of movements deployed within it.'

Michel de Certeau [10]

In a way all three of these artworks invite us to question the city – its democratic promises and commercial interests. Rather than facilitate these interests, Shaw and Payot took up an observing, interpreting and analysing role, positioned slightly off-stage, or in the 'gods', rather than centre-stage organising everybody. They are creating alternative guidebooks or manuals of Preston (with fragments of information about its population, fashion, history), offering information for visitors, planners and residents to get another sense of the city. These projects aren't trying to orchestrate patronising pantomimes of social cohesion, they are merely showing the existing stories of the city – in all their messy, unpredictable, colourful, oppressive glory! Rather than activating spaces, they are drawing attention to the current inactions and actions of the people moving through them.

'The crowd is the veil through which the familiar city is transformed for the flâneur into phantasmagoria. The phantasmagoria, in which the city appears now as a landscape, now as a room, seems later to have inspired the décor of department stores, which thus put flânerie to work for profit. In any case, department stores are the last precincts of flânerie.'

Walter Benjamin[11]

While the Cenotaph and Lune Street monuments are testimonies of a moment in history, *Local Colour* and *Supervised* offer a different type of sculptural remain for future generations of Preston. They might not be so weighty, in material and event, but they capture ephemeral aspects of parts of the city that are no less physical. *Local Colour* is composed of garments that have travelled half way around the world, some manufactured in factories that employ working conditions that might have been familiar to the striking workers of the Preston cotton mills in the 1840s. There are not necessarily soldiers pointing guns at the working classes in Preston anymore, but inequality certainly still exists on both a local and global scale. The distinction between the oppressed and oppressor so clearly defined in Young's 1992 sculpture is perhaps less obvious now, as we willingly buy the cheap clothes that keep down wages in other parts of the world. While *Local Colour* and *Supervised* don't ask us to remember a certain moment, versions of the urban fabric are presented as mock-ups of research and data observed about the life of a city. These logs, charts and traces of the body politics of Preston raise questions about how we measure, map, predict, plan as well as survive in a city. The individuals moving through these spaces create patchworks and cacophonies of sound and colour. In Certain Places and the artists they work with are carefully navigating a critical path through these 'stories-so-far', creating comforting, disturbing and constantly unfolding scenarios on the city's stage.

1. Doreen Massey, *For Space*, Sage, 2005, p.9.

2. *Synecdoche, New York* (2008) directed by Charlie Kauffman.

3. Jeroen Boomgaard, *Wild Park: Commissioning the Unexpected*, Fonds Voor Beeldende Kunsten, Vormgeving & Bouwkunst, 2012, p.23.

4. 'New survey reveals children's deprivation', *Lancashire Evening Post*, 16 October 2008.

5. Tom McCarthy, *Remainder*, Metronome Press, 2005, Vintage, 2006, p.88.

6. Louis-Auguste Blanqui quoted in Walter Benjamin, 'Paris, Capital of the Nineteenth Century, Expose of 1939', in *The Arcades Project*, Harvard University Press edition, 2002, p.26.

7. See http://trendfashion1.wordpress.com/.

8. See http://www.colormarketing.org/Media.aspx?id=913&.

9. Greg Smith, 'Mediated Cityscapes 02: Memory and the City', http://www.creativeapplications.net/theory/mediated-cityscapes-02-memory-and-the-city/.

10. Michel de Certeau, *The Practice of Everyday Life*, University of California Press, 1984, p.117.

11. Walter Benjamin, op. cit., p.21.

FASHIONISTAS: Artist Becky Shaw, right, with her artwork and Miss Matilda's Boutique proprietor Emma Almond
Pictures: DAVID HURST

She's a dedicated follower of fashion

Artist captures changing shop window

by Suzanne Harvey
suzanne.harvey@lep.co.uk

ARTIST Becky Shaw has been trawling the streets of Preston snapping every item of women's clothing on the high street.

Over the past three months, she has visited the city centre to chart the changes in the shop windows.

Each image was then arranged on to a montage, mapping the colours and textures as they change from summer to autumn.

And now shoppers can pick up the free, limited edition prints – called Local Colour – when they visit boutiques around the city until October.

Becky said: "I'm really fascinated with shop windows and how they reflect our identity.

"I became interested after shop-

CHANGING SEASONS: Artist Becky Shaw

The pictures are available from: AJ'Z Boardwear, Miller Arcade; The Closet, Guildhall Street; DB3, The Mall; Duncans Designer Clothing, Crystal House; Fusion, The Mall; Melange Lifestyle, Fishergate Centre; Miss Matilda's Boutique, Winck-

ley Street; Novello, Fisherga Reef Clothing, The Mall; Re The Mall; O'Neill, The Mall; Temptation, Fishergate Centr

video
lep.co.uk

Local Art for Local People
Becky Shaw

In 2002 I visited the Tatsurou Bashi work *Villa Victoria* (commissioned for the Liverpool Biennial), which built a modern hotel room around the Victoria monument in Liverpool. As I walked up the entrance gangway I overheard a series of elderly Scousers talking about the work. One group talked about changing sexual morality, another talked about the history and how currents of thought re-emerge from the past and live in the present, and another talked about tourism in Liverpool. All these complicated ideas, and many others, were being articulated in one moment, in one work, in one city. Nothing I saw in the rest of the Biennial impressed me as much as the thoughts generated by this work. This work needed no explanatory text and no education programme (and I'm not at all against these things). Quite simply, the work was intelligent and its physical qualities were delivered with conviction. The evident concentration on the quality of realisation meant that the idea embedded in the work was articulate, without being laboured, and it generated a complex response from an audience of locals and visitors. After seeing this, the rest of the Biennial seemed unnecessary.

The Victoria monument work questioned the logic of the Biennial festival as a place to experience art. Obviously Biennials are about more than art – they are intended to accelerate tourism and boost the retail and service industry. However, as a visitor, *Villa Victoria* gave me much more to 'go home with' than the many smaller works that appeared scattered around the city, or the works in the galleries. The experience made me think about the difference between encountering a single commissioned sited work, and encountering works in a festival.

In Certain Places in general sites one work at a time in Preston, orchestrating all of their resources to realise one thing well, in one public situation. It always seems contrary to me that we save our 'best' art for galleries and sometimes exact different standards for art in the public realm. Take, for example, the art we see in hospitals. Hospitals, like cities, house all sorts of people, but it is all too often assumed that these people, the 'locals', will like their art easy to digest. Obviously, what art can be seen, and where, is limited by finance. More than this, the quality of art in public spaces is due to the ambition and quality of the commissioner or curator. However, the debate about quality (and quality *is* always an argument or a debate, rather than a set of unchanging criteria) is often sidelined by anxiety about accessibility or relevance. 'Relevance' assumes that art that 'people will understand' is democratic. Frank Skinner, for me, sums this up with his phrase, 'local is a euphemism for crap', defining an attitude of 'low horizons' towards a home populace. However, to focus on the quality of the artwork and its precise delivery is much more democratic than any lowest common denominator of public understanding.

To assume less of people is undemocratic. Putting great art in public places assumes the best of the place and its residents – it understands that they are up for the debate.

In the past twenty years 'temporary', 'contingent' or 'provisional' became bywords in public realm commissioning. Some of this stemmed from the critical turn of relationism, focused upon encounter and experience. While there were many significant works of this kind, the zeitgeist offered an interesting frame for local commissioning. On the one hand intelligent councils could see the engaging potential of works that were form-light, but on the other hand it was easy for these works to become a get-out for local bodies fearful of the negative press of expensive permanent works. While this perhaps saved us from some of the worse cases of traffic-island sculpture, it also offered a way to be non-committal. By funding projects that 'engaged' instead of offering indisputable aesthetic positions, councils could assert the value of their commissions in a language they were more familiar with. However, the singular work, well realised in the public realm, like *Villa Victoria*, or the Jeppe Hein fountain in Preston, offered a breath of fresh air in a commitment-phobic environment. The works were not permanent, but they were realised like they were – with a focus on getting it right and thinking carefully about every bit of the form. These works were intent upon making their mark instead of being scared of their own impact, or in the word of the green movement, their 'footprint'.

In Certain Places commissions art mostly one at a time, and rarely as part of a festival. There is no tourist trail involving looking for artworks on a map. That's not to say that there is no interest in how culture can extend or develop a place, rather there is a chain of encounters. Coming into contact with an artwork with or without a festival is a very different experience. Without the festival the viewer has no frame to isolate the art in, and the art has no fellow works to build a bigger picture. The viewer also has to deal with the art in their space, a space that hasn't been framed or identified by a cultural body.

The 'frameless' encounter means two things: that the artist can realise a work where its boundaries can be built according to the context, rather than where it bangs up against someone else's art. It also means that the art and artist have to work really hard to either understand or negotiate where the edges of the work begin and end. When I made *Local Colour* I wasn't sure where the 'space' of the work was. The process involved walking the entire high street once a month, for three months, taking a photographic sample of every different women's garment in every shop window. The work began from my curiosity about how international colour trend prediction processes related to the specificity of local supply and demand. My curiosity had been generated by visiting different Topshops in different cities, noticing that the Topshop in Preston had more navy blue than the one in Sheffield.

Once the photographic samples had been collected, they were printed through a high-street commercial photographic developer, after which a sample was hand-cut and the samples tiled into 'trend prediction' tables based on the ones produced at Première Vision, a fabric trend forecasting agency in Paris. By making the tables by hand, I felt like it was my collection, and I owned it – so the samples went on the same journey as if they were garments I had bought. Normally we can only buy one, or a few garments, but this way I had consumed the whole high street. The prints were distributed through shopping bags, to be read and viewed at home. At home the shopper remembers, again, that they have only bought a garment, not an aspiration. The prints were issued once a month for three months, trying to capture the changing retail season: enthusiasm for summer, the slump into 'Sales' malaise and then the refreshment of the autumn palette. This timetable, though, meant the work unfolded over time, and the expectation that people might get all three was maybe ambitious.

To realise a single work in a site, the artist, the curatorial team, and the artwork must work really hard to be articulate. Single works in a site are encountered through the context of the place, whereas in a festival the place is also framed by all the other work. The works commissioned by In Certain Places contribute to wider dialogue about art in the public realm, however at point of encounter they can't rely on an external validation, so they live or die at the moment of their local experience. The artist and curatorial team must also understand what it means when things don't work out as planned. Things 'going wrong' is sometimes a sign that the context and its relationship to art is being made tangible. When I was taking the photographs for *Local Colour*, the second time I walked through the shopping centre, the security guards were waiting for me. I tried to take

the photos discreetly, even pretending I was on my mobile while browsing. But in the end the pressure was too much and I had to give up. I had to find a solution to the missing images, so instead I counted every garment and clicked my shutter the same number of times, with my hand over the lens, so I got a run of black samples. Strangely, when I went back for July, no guards followed me and I was able to get the samples. I imagine they thought the work had been finished or ended so they were no longer 'on guard'. This moment could have meant that the work had failed, but instead, it allowed some of the situation to bleed in, and to upset the conceit of the conceptual framework. In *Essays on the Blurring of Art and Life* (1993) Allan Kaprow refers to a social skin, a 'meniscus', that the artist pushes against when they make work. The 'meniscus' is a useful visual metaphor: a plastic membrane that can be pushed and punctuated. What I like about the 'meniscus' is that is two-way – the liquid of social life flows forwards and can push back.

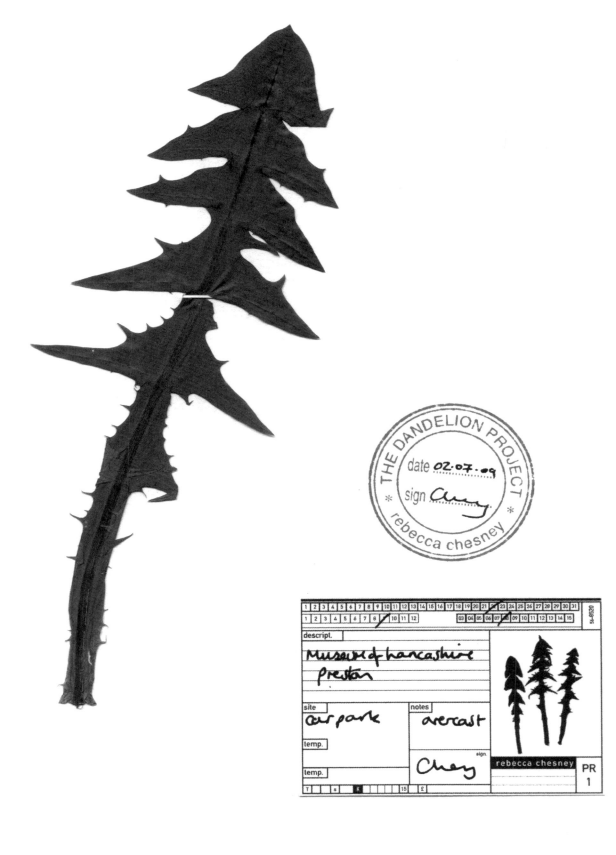

THE DANDELION PROJECT

date 02·07·09

sign *Amy*

rebecca chesney

1	2	3	4	5	6	7	8	9	10	11	12	13	14	15	16	17	18	19	20	21	22	23	24	25	26	27	28	29	30	31
1	2	3	4	5	6	7	8		10	11	12								03	04	05	06	07	08	09	10	11	12	13	14	15

56-8520

descript.

Museum of Lancashire
Preston

site
car park

notes
overcast

temp.

temp.

sign. Chery

rebecca chesney

PR
1

| T | | a | K | | | | 15 | £ | |

Place beyond Place
Elaine Speight

Along one of the quiet lanes, which branch off from Preston's high street and descend towards the river, there is a small delivery bay at the back of Boots the Chemist. Beneath the store's concertinaed goods door, around a metre below eye level, is a small, royal blue oval plaque, reminiscent of those installed by English Heritage to commemorate the residence or workplace of distinguished historical figures. Contrasting against the blue, in a white sans serif font, the plaque simply states, 'An accountant sheltered here', and below, in smaller text, are the words 'Invisible Skills'. Similar plaques can be found in other doorways and hidden locations across the city, marking the sheltering spots of a midwife, doctor, footballer, cleaner, lorry driver and dancer, among others. Part of a project, entitled *Significant Other* (2012), by Susan Walsh, the plaques are temporary memorials to the many people who, at some point in their lives, find themselves sleeping rough, and an acknowledgement of their, overlooked, contributions to a place.

Although In Certain Places did not commission this artwork, it provides a powerful example of how artists in the programme have engaged with the city as a site of human experience and complex social relations.[1] Preston's history is shaped by the movements of people, and imbued with their knowledge, memories, practices and beliefs. Yet, like all places, the experiences and ideas of certain individuals and social groups have a far more visible presence than the experience and ideas of others. For a number of artists – including Walsh, who also created an earlier artwork as part of In Certain Places – the programme has provided an opportunity to reveal some of these hidden narratives, and to celebrate the roles that they continue to play within the everyday life of the city. At the same time, these artworks have exposed some of the threads that tie Preston to other locations, raising questions about its role within an increasingly globalised world.

Doreen Massey describes places as 'collections of stories-so-far', which are articulated within 'the wider power-geometries of space'.[2] Accordingly, the character of a city can be thought of as the result of the 'meeting and weaving together' of such stories, which, in turn, connect to other people, places and times.[3] As a post-industrial city, Preston is both the product and producer of social connections that stretch out across the globe. Every 20 years, the city sends out its Guild Scrolls to amass messages of goodwill from its émigrés in countries such as Canada or New Zealand, and communities with strong familial ties to the city in Pakistan, India, the Caribbean, and, more recently, China. The Harris Museum & Art Gallery is also a testament to its historic global links. A repository of ornaments, paintings, textiles and sculptures from locations across the world, the building embodies the imperialist values upon which modern Preston was built. *The Gates of Paradise* (2012) – a sound piece and performance by Collaborative Space – focused on the Harris's connection with cities throughout Europe and the United States, as the home to one of eighteen cast copies of the Baptistery doors in Florence. Mimicking the popular guided tours of European cities, the performance addressed issues of authenticity, ownership and the perceived ability of such objects to enlighten the working classes. Shezad Dawood's film and exhibition *Piercing Brightness* (2011/12) was also informed by artefacts within the museum's collection. The nineteenth-century pattern books, which inspired his work, are beautiful, yet disquieting objects. Exquisite samples of woven, printed and embroidered textiles collected by the taxonomist John Forbes Watson during his travels across South Asia, these books provided patterns for British industrialists, who subsequently flooded the Asian market with their cheaper reproductions.

Despite its diminutive size, Preston is a network of power relations that continue to affect other places in profound, and sometimes troubling ways. Becky Shaw's project, *Local Colour* (2008), illustrates the rapid rate of product turnover and consumption, which, even post-recession, characterises the high street and damages the living conditions and health of workers overseas. Meanwhile Dawood's references to UFOs were inspired by the high level of sightings in the area that are commonly attributed to the activities of British Aerospace. One of the largest employers in the area, the company has a history of supplying arms to the governments of countries such as Zimbabwe and Saudi Arabia, with poor human rights records. Although few of the artworks have engaged with such political issues directly, by emphasising the expanded nature of the city, they have helped us to understand it outside a purely local context, and provoked questions about its responsibilities to other people in the world.

If places are the product of social relations, then it follows that they can be dysfunctional as well as dynamic. Indeed, Massey points out that the specificities of a place are equally informed by 'the non-meeting-ups, the disconnections and the relationships not established'.[4] For Pam Holmes, these absences formed the subject of her work. Despite constituting over ten per cent of the city's population, Prestonians of African and Caribbean descent are barely visible within its centre. By pasting portraits of black and mixed-race residents on the city's advertising boards, her project *Beside the Seaside…* (2006) drew attention to the under-representation of such groups, while also challenging attitudes towards identity and place. Reminiscent of Ingrid Pollard's *Pastoral Interlude* (1988), in which solitary black figures are depicted in idyllic countryside scenes, Holmes's photographs were taken in the nearby coastal resort of Blackpool. Pictured in settings more commonly associated with white working-class people at play, her subjects disrupt traditional notions of local identity and question what it means to 'belong' to a place within the contemporary globalised world.

The question of belonging can also be identified in other artworks in the programme. Inspired by the work of the Sophie Lancaster Foundation, which campaigns to protect subculture groups against hate crimes, Iain Broadley's *The Black Parade* (2012) assembled people who identified as part of an 'alternative' culture to participate in the community processions that took place during the Guild. Many of these participants were teenagers, who congregate around a city-centre landmark called the Peace Garden to skateboard, chat and flirt. Regarded as a nuisance by some other users of the space, these young people exist on the social periphery of the city – often too young to have a voice in its governance, and lacking the financial resources to be the consumers it requires. By encouraging them to assert their civic identities as part of a wider group, *The Black Parade* legitimised their presence in the streets and demanded that they be recognised as equal members of Preston's community.

While places may be increasingly fluid and connected, the stigmatisation of such groups shows that cultural and social boundaries continue to exist. Moreover, as new immigrants and international students arrive on the streets of Preston, the feeling of being 'out of place' is surely a common one. Magda Stawarska-Beavan's sound piece, *The Arcade* (2010), was informed by her double sense of displacement, from both the Polish town that she left as a young woman, and the city she has lived in for over a decade. The artwork, which brought the sounds of Kraków's main square into the Harris Museum & Art Gallery, demonstrated the ability of 'outsiders' to generate new perspectives on a place. Similarly, Susan Walsh's film *To Scatter* (2010) explored the significance of music and song for the collective memory of displaced people, and celebrated the cultural contributions to the city that migrants continue to make.

As part of the 'Place beyond Place' symposium in 2010, curator Paul Goodwin spoke about the relationships between minority cultural communities and the form and functions of the city. Specifically, he outlined the concept of 'Black Urbanism' as a way to think about alternative models of inhabiting a place, which are informed by the creativity and cultures of different ethnic groups. At the same event, artist Rebecca Chesney also reminded us that the stigma of being 'out of place' is not confined to the human world. Her *Tanpopo Tour* led delegates around the backstreets and 'weed hotspots' of Preston. Examining how and why plants from across the globe thrive within the city, the tour also questioned the notion of 'invasive', 'exotic' and 'alien' species, pointing out, for example, that the humble dandelion is as troublesome in Japan as Japanese knotweed is here.

The movement of people, ideas, goods and money is central to the economic survival of a city. However, as geographer Tim Cresswell points out, mobility is entangled with meaning and power, and 'the production of some kinds of mobility often effectively immobilizes others'.[5] While, for some people, mobility is enforced, the movement of others is often restricted. As communications and transport technologies grow ever faster and efficient, it is tempting to believe that everyone is more connected and mobile than ever. In 2007, when Blast Theory brought their mixed-reality game to Preston, the Internet was nowhere near as pervasive as it is in our lives today. However, as Prestonians chased players in Tokyo and São Paulo around the familiar city streets, it felt as if the world had become a much more intimate place. As the project has developed, however, we have come to realise that, despite being globally connected, for some people living in Preston it can also be an isolating place.

The Family project (2007), in particular, challenged our preconceptions of the city. Developed by artist Chris Davis, the project introduced us to Pam Moores and her family, who live in the city's Ribbleton area. Without a car, and over two miles north of the centre, travelling into Preston can be difficult for Pam. Moreover, as a middle-aged woman, its quieter parts, such as Avenham Park, are 'no go' areas for her. Through the use of Skype – an online tool more commonly used to connect people hundreds of miles apart – we were able to develop a dialogue about our different perceptions of place. By creating a 'neutral' space between her living room and Charles Quick's university office, the technology also facilitated a long-term conversation about the role of artists in a city. Through discussions with the artists we commissioned, Pam gained an insight into our processes and practice, and advised us how to better connect with people who live outside of the city centre.

For Massey, acknowledging the global power relations that constitute a place is the basis for developing a progressive type of politics, which 'looks from the inside out'.[6] Described as a politics of 'place beyond place', this approach 'recognises not just… the "outside" that can be found within, but also… the "inside" that lies beyond'. The challenge for a city, therefore, is to develop a more responsible global outlook by attending to the existing social relations of which it is produced.

As its cultural make-up continues to shift and, particularly through the university's involvement with countries such as China, its international reach expands, a politics of 'place beyond place' is increasingly vital for Preston. By uncovering the cultural narratives and contributions, which it often overlooks, and tracing its threads of influence upon other lives across the world, the artworks we have commissioned present an expanded sense of place. As such, they provide a starting point for considering the everyday realities of globalisation, and generating conversations about Preston's place in the world.

1. *Significant Other* was created as part of the 'Moments That Matter – Trophy Cups' exhibition by Lubaina Himid. The exhibition was a collaboration between WE PLAY EXPO, Harris Museum & Art Gallery, and artists Lubaina Himid, Rebecca Chesney, Susan Walsh and Denise Swanson.

2. Doreen Massey, *For Space*, Sage Publications Ltd., 2005, p.130.

3. Doreen Massey, *Space, Place and Gender*, University of Minnesota Press, 1994, p.154.

4. Massey, *For Space*, p.130.

5. Tim Creswell, *On the Move: Mobility in the Western World*, Routledge, 2006, p.260.

6. Doreen Massey, *World City,* Polity, 2007, p.193.

Blast Theory, *Can You See Me Now?*, Guild Hall shopping arcade, Brew Cafe, Bruccianis Cafe and Preston city centre

Can You See Me Now? is a chase game which is played simultaneously on the Internet and in real city streets. The game explores the impact that new technologies can have in a city and their potential to offer new experiences of the urban environment. Through a series of research visits to the city, Blast Theory created a 3D virtual representation of Preston city centre, which formed the basis of the game. Over two days in July 2007, people across the globe were able to explore the city's streets and landmarks by logging on to the Web and participating in the game. While these players moved through the virtual streets of Preston, 'runners', tracked by satellites, chased them across the real city centre.

Can You See Me Now? brought the world to Preston, and players from as far afield as Brazil and Saudi Arabia logged on to explore the city. Closer to home, people could play the game on computer terminals, which were set up in the Guild Hall shopping arcade and in city centre cafes. Although the game has been played in a number of other locations, including Tokyo and Seattle, the Preston version attracted the greatest number of 'hits' the game had ever received.

July 2007

Chris Davis, *The Family*, Preston city centre, Brookfield Estate, Online

The Family was a creative evaluation of In Certain Places' work, which was developed by artist Chris Davis, working alongside the Moores Family on the Brookfield Estate in the north of Preston. In 2007, Chris installed a computer in the Moores' family home, to enable them to talk, via a video-chat facility, with the artists, curators and other participants in the In Certain Places project.

The Moores were able to witness and have a direct input into a range of temporary public artworks that took place in Preston city centre during the time frame of the project. This opportunity enabled the family, who live on the periphery of Preston, to become involved in the commissioning process. Through discussions with the curatorial team, they were able to raise issues about their needs and how they perceive the In Certain Places project to affect their cultural, social and physical world in relation to the planned redevelopment of Preston's public realm.

This dialogue formed a cultural exchange, which broadened understandings of the issues that both parties have to address on a daily basis in the city. The conversations were recorded and edited to produce a film, which was projected onto a shop window in the Guild Hall shopping arcade during a week in February 2008.

May 2007–December 2008

The Family

I've never liked art, you know, but now it's alright... Chris asked me to do *The Family* project... We've been going out and looking at art, public art, and telling him what I think. The other people in my family like to have a say and get involved, especially my granddaughter, Rosie, she comes and chats to Charles.

[About *Appearing Rooms*] – it was nice – everybody was going into the water, running in and out, and it was packed with people watching, and they felt safe and everything.

Pam Moores

From my perspective, it's good that Pam's getting involved in the project, and there are practical benefits in terms of having a new computer system to use and things like that. But also, it's about her engaging with other people who call themselves artists and arts officers who organise the art, and looking at the whole process, rather than just looking at a piece of art. She's involved in how it all happens, which I think is of as much interest as the actual production of the thing.

Chris Davis

Audience feedback

I think it's good art... different, I didn't really think that art could be like this... it's good how stuff like this is happening in Preston.

I heard a right Lancashire accent and I thought 'what's that'? So I stopped to look at it, it's really good isn't it? These are local people not actors. I like that.

Collaborative Space, *The Gates of Paradise*, Harris Museum & Art Gallery

The Gates of Paradise is an ongoing research project, which connects Preston with other locations around the world. The project centres on the Gates of Paradise, which are housed in the Harris Museum & Art Gallery and are one of eighteen cast copies of the original doors of the Baptistery in Florence.

Collaborative Space is a creative partnership led by Jeni McConnell and Hannah Elizabeth Allan. Their project reflected upon the relationship between Preston and Florence, transposing and navigating one space through another, exploring the dialogue of light, sound and sensation between the two locations. An audio piece, using recordings made around the Gates and Duomo Square in Florence, was played once a day during the week of the 2012 Preston Guild. This was accompanied by two live performances, in which the artists evoked the sights, sounds and tastes of Florence within the Harris Museum's rotunda. Audiences were encouraged to think differently about Preston: to reassess how they understand and negotiate their experiences in the city, and reflect on visiting another place.

September 2012

Jeni McConnell

Before I started the Fine Art MA at UCLan, they joined the two pathways, 'Site and Place' and 'Archive Intervention'. To me, it felt very important that the two were together, as they related to very significant parts of my practice. So, it was that interest in the course that initially connected me with In Certain Places. During my MA I went to different In Certain Places events, because they were relevant to my practice. Since then, I've helped out with other events.

Hannah Allan, Nicola Martin and I put an application in to the 2012 Guild, proposing to do a project in which we looked at cast copies of the Gates of Paradise, and their European and American connections. We didn't get the funding, but it sparked the idea that maybe In Certain Places could do something for the Guild.

I think Charles was the instigator of thinking about the Gates, because he told me that there was a cast copy in the Harris Museum in Preston. As most people say, when you walk into the cafe at the Harris Museum, you don't see them. The building is a bit overwhelming, because there are a lot of big things, and maybe people see them as being part of the architecture rather than actually being an artwork.

Finding that history of it: discovering how it's connected to the Victoria & Albert Museum, how they purchased it, how they transported it, how it lay waiting for the Harris Museum to open, and, once the museum had opened, how it was fixed to the walls... Why did they need a copy of this thing? It was interesting, once we started working on it, doing the research and going to places like Berlin. For me the history of each place was also interesting, particularly in Berlin, because they've preserved the scars of war.

The group review sessions arranged with external curators were really helpful. I think that we were all a bit nervous, but it makes you realise that they're just normal people. Maybe those conversations shifted the project slightly and shaped the eventual outcome.

Iain Broadley, *The Black Parade*, Preston city centre

The Black Parade was a participatory art project, which celebrated alternative cultures in and around Preston. This celebration made a statement of intent on behalf of subculture groups; not to be 'tolerated' on the outskirts of culture, treated as 'freaks' or 'outsiders', but accepted as part of a society, in which difference is often treated with contempt.

Throughout August 2012, Broadley worked with young people to develop alternative floats for the community and torchlight processions, as part of the Preston Guild. Produced in collaboration with the Sophie Lancaster Foundation, which represents people who view themselves as part of an alternative culture, *The Black Parade* formed part of a wider movement to bring about a change within mainstream society, presenting alternative life choices as the 'noise in teeth gritting harmony of society'.[1]

September 2012

1. Dick Hebdige, *The Meaning of Style*, Routledge, 1979.

Magda Stawarska-Beavan, *The Arcade*, Harris Museum & Art Gallery

The Arcade is a sound piece that brought the soundscape of Rynek Główny, the main square in Kraków, Poland, to the Harris Museum & Art Gallery. The recording was made in the Sukiennice, an arcaded Renaissance cloth hall, the origins of which date from 1257, and illustrates a day in the life of Rynek Główny. It begins at the moment the city awakens, with birdsong, the footsteps of people going to work, cleaning machines, early maintenance and building work, and it ends with tourists and locals making their way home from bars and clubs. Each hour is marked by a chiming clock in Rynek Główny and a trumpet signal, played from one of two towers in the square. The tune breaks off in mid-stream to commemorate a thirteenth-century trumpeter, who was shot while sounding the alarm during an attack on the city.

The interaction of visitors with the sound and architecture was an important element of the work, and the piece held specific meanings for different audiences. For a Polish immigrant the sound of the trumpet player from Mariacki Church may have provoked nostalgia and perhaps longing for the familiar sounds of the motherland, while the noise of a busy arcade transported a local Preston audience to a more recent past, when the city was a lively bustling centre of commerce.

April 2010

Magda Stawarska-Beavan

Lubaina [Himid] and I went for a long walk around Preston and she showed me different places she was interested in. Of course, I was familiar with Preston, but she showed me another place. After that I went away and started thinking about different sites that I could work with. It was an interesting way to explore the city.

When we were walking, we were talking about Polish communities in Preston and how Polish communities had been in the North West for years, as immigrants after World War II, and then a larger flux of Polish immigrants came when Poland joined the European Union.

What is really interesting with a sound piece is that, because you don't have a visual image, you start reading the sound depending on where it is. I was trying to think about the passage of time and how a place changes during the course of the day. So, by playing the piece in that location [the cafe at the Harris Museum & Art Gallery] you start noticing things that you haven't noticed before. For example, there are two clocks in the centre of the cafe, so you start looking at the references to time almost as if they've been placed there on purpose. Then there are the relief images of horses, which run around the inside of the building, which comes through when you hear the sounds of horses repeatedly in the course of the day. It was very exciting for me to be able to edit something in a studio and then to present it in a dimension where it gained a completely different meaning.

The piece changes depending on the environment in which it's played and that is important for how the piece is read. You observe a place differently when you're from somewhere else. I feel like I'm not local anywhere, because I don't feel local when I go home to see my parents either. My parents have been living in what I would call my hometown since I was 9 and I emigrated when I was 20, so I'm not really attached to any location. I think that's what interests me about experiencing a place.

To me, it was interesting to experience the layers of one location, which was very close to me, in Preston where I've been living for such a long time. I was hoping that maybe I could evoke the experience for some of the visitors to the Harris. I think quite a lot of the Polish community walk through the cafe to use the Internet in the library.

It was really beneficial to see my work in a different way. Also, being put in the same context as other artists that you work with probably made me a bit braver to try to think in a wider context.

Magda Stawarska-Beavan
THE ARCADE

23rd April - 6th May 2010 9.30am-5.30pm, Miller Arcade, Church Street, Preston

Pam Holmes, *Beside the Seaside...*, Preston city centre

Pam Holmes, an artist who uses photography, worked with black and mixed-race Lancashire residents to produce a series of three images, which were displayed on billboards at key entry points in Preston. The images, which were taken in Blackpool, focused on the traditional English setting of the seaside and created docudramas, which aimed to deconstruct the myth of England and the notion of Englishness.

July 2006

Place beyond Place

'Place beyond Place' was a one-day symposium, which brought together urban planners, artists, architects, urban designers and people with an interest in cities. Inspired by geographer Doreen Massey's 'politics of place beyond place', which acknowledges the global relations and responsibilities of a place, the symposium used Preston as a context within which to examine the complex relationships between the local and the global.

Hosted in an empty shop, the event included presentations by artist Loraine Leeson and curator and urban theorist Paul Goodwin, alongside tours of the city by artists Rebecca Chesney, William Titley, Catriona Stamp and Emma Heslewood, Keeper of History at the Harris Museum & Art Gallery.

Rebecca Chesney, *Tanpopo Tour*

Preston is host to intruders, aliens and escaped chancers – thriving alongside natives in back streets and adapting to the harsh, inhospitable conditions of the urban landscape. Have these inhabitants always been resident? Are they accidental tourists or perhaps the offspring of invited guests?

In 2006 Chesney conducted a weed survey of Preston city centre that revealed over 70 different plant species within the urban environment. With dandelions being one of the most common species in the city, Chesney began to further investigate the plant. Her research led her to Japan, where the European dandelion *Taraxacum officinale* is now considered an alien invasive species that is eradicating its native counterpart *Taraxacum japonicum*. The *Tanpopo Tour* of

Preston took participants to some of the city's weed hotspots – revealing how plant species from all over the world have come to settle in this unlikely habitat.

Emma Heslewood, *The World through Avenham*

Emma Heslewood's tour explored some of the global stories connected with Preston's first Victorian 'suburb' Avenham; an area that has nurtured new inventions, ideas and faiths, yet also felt the full impact of economic and social change.

William Titley, *Here & There*

William Titley's tour explored the idea of hybrid space by navigating Preston using a map from Lahore, Pakistan. The physical negotiation of Preston, mixed with the artist's own memory of Lahore created a new, virtual space in the minds of his participants. By meandering 'here' and describing 'there', the tour challenged experiences of place, and produced new encounters with the city through walking, talking and the imagination.

Catriona Stamp, *Banks and Buskers –*
Contrasting Threads Making the Fabric of Fishergate

Catriona Stamp's tour examined the threads of time and the interplay of global influences, which collectively create Preston's high street, by looking at the stories behind some of the buildings on Fishergate.

April 2010

Place beyond Place

Stimulating intellectual debate followed
by a lovely and interesting walk. Good
to escape the office and put our
work into a wider context, and to be
reminded of the academic rigour that
can and is applied and is continually
developing around public art.

It opened my eyes to new notions
around place shaping.

The talks were really interesting, but
I especially enjoyed the tour around
Preston – it felt more relaxed – it
was easy to talk to people and I got
to see Preston from an interesting
new point of view.

Shezad Dawood, *Piercing Brightness*, Various locations in Preston

Piercing Brightness is a science fiction film, which formed the outcome of a two-and-a half-year relationship between Shezad Dawood, In Certain Places, and the people and places of Preston. Using familiar landmarks and locations across the city, the film tells the story of Shin and Jiang, a young Chinese man and woman, sent from another planet to retrieve the 'Glorious 100' – members of an alien race, who, countless generations ago, were sent to Earth to study and observe. Living through many lives without any scope for return, some have become corrupted, forgetting their original purpose and slowly becoming influenced by, and in turn influencing, their adopted home.

The story takes place on the streets of Preston and climaxes with a dramatic car chase, which ends on the roof of Preston's controversial brutalist Bus Station. The Preston flavour of the film is further enhanced by the involvement of local people, who feature alongside familiar faces including Tracy Brabin and Bhasker Patel. Preston actress Samantha Edwards stars as one of the central characters, and over 70 people from the city feature as extras in scenes that were filmed in the city's parks, shops, square and nightclubs, and an abandoned cinema and post office.

Dawood describes the concept of *Piercing Brightness* as a creative hybrid of *My Beautiful Laundrette* and *Roswell*. Following its premiere in 2012, as part of the Preston Guild celebrations, it was distributed to cinemas across the UK and internationally, bringing Preston to the world. It has also recently been released on DVD and blu-ray.

Piercing Brightness was commissioned in association with Modern Art Oxford and with further support of Abandon Normal Devices Festival and Outset Contemporary Art Fund. The film was accompanied by an exhibition of new prints, textile and neon works by Dawood, which premiered at the Harris Museum & Art Gallery in September 2011, and toured to Modern Art Oxford and Newling Art Gallery and The Exchange. The film and the exhibitions were accompanied by a book with the same title.

July 2011–September 2012

Shezad Dawood

It's not the first film that I have made that has a relationship to a place. For me that's a real staring point, and it is not that I set out to make a documentary by any means. In a way a documentary feels like just a question-answer format, like that idea of true perspective. I feel uncomfortable with the idea that anything is true, so to try and make a true picture of a place interests me less than getting to know a place and make a fantastical picture.

... the people, the institutions and the place collaborate on something, and for me to have the extras from the places gives a certain reality to what you are doing. It comes alive, and in a way they become representatives of the larger city and its workings. It does become a quasi-documentary, and I like the fact that it has this documentary aspect, but ends up as such a fantastical narrative.

That goes back to some of the research that went into the film, like the idea that Lancashire has such a high UFO sighting rate, which can easily be explained by the fact that BAE systems is in Lancashire. Equally, Preston having the fastest growing mainland Chinese population in Britain, simply because UCLan was the first British university to have an annexe in China. So this relationship between fantastical and the very grounded and real is really interesting to me.

When we went to meet the public relations director of the Church of Jesus Christ of the Latter Day Saints (Mormons), finding out that the first mass Mormon baptism took place in the River Ribble, and that Preston suddenly had all this energy or layering of history, that was so rich. Then there were the mill workers' uprisings throughout all these different histories, each one quite substantial on its own. To have all these strands converge in Preston suddenly gave a richness, like a banquet or backbone to the film, and it became of here and from here.

Piercing Brightness

I was approached, completely out of the blue on the street while I was working – I sell the *Big Issue* outside Marks & Spencer in Preston – and was asked if I would like to be in a science fiction movie as an extra. So I said 'most definitely, yes'. The most memorable moment for me would be outside the disused cinema on Fishergate, where me and an Asian guy had to surreptitiously sneak into the secret alien meeting in the cinema. The camera was on me, only for a few seconds, and it was on the other guy, as we walked in through all that debris and saw how disused it all was – the perfect location. The fact that the camera was on me, and I was surrounded by 150, shall we say 'partygoers', queuing for the nightclubs, you had that live kind of feeling. I thought, 'I can't make a mistake here'. I wanted to try my best. The people around were fantastic.

Bradley Clarke

When I saw the advert in a shopping arcade, I was a bit hesitant at first, because I probably thought that this was mostly a film for younger people. But then I thought, with any film you need quite a broad age range, from young to elderly, and so I thought 'alright, great, I'm going to go in and give an audition and see how I do'... You get an insight into what is happening behind the camera – there's quite a lot to see really, it's very enjoyable. So that's why I did it. Originally, I had one role as a bartender, but then I was asked if I would mind playing a role called the White Robe. It's basically an alien. So I went in with an open mind and I played the part of an alien, visiting this planet... There was so much that I really enjoyed. It was the knowledge that people were actually making a film about this story, and it's an incredible story – it's the mystery suspense, they're not sure what's really happening. Just being there, the crew were fantastic, it was really enjoyable...

Malcolm Langley

Feedback

I was in three scenes. The first was in the old Odeon cinema. It was quite breathtaking when I went in there, as I didn't realise there was anywhere like that. The second was the big park scene, where we were walking towards the UFO. The third and final scene I actually had a line in, which was quite nice. That was the pub scene with the UFO enthusiast group. I didn't expect to get a line at all. I honestly expected some drama students to get it, not one of the volunteer extras. It was a real pleasure to get that, and it was a pleasure to work with the professional actors. They actually complimented me, and everyone else who had lines in that scene, because all the people round the table were extras.

I haven't done any acting since primary school, but I do have a hobby called 'live action role play'. I am a creative person. I'm working on several things, but this was slightly different. This one line I had to do just right. With a little bit of interpretation from me – just to make it unique to the character... I loved every minute. OK, it over-ran a lot of the time. That particular scene where I had lines, it was 4 in the morning when we finished!

I would actually remember it as a good experience and a slightly bad one. The good one was that it was just such a wonderful to be involved in. The bad one, I must insist, if ever you see anyone drinking – in *Coronation Street*, or any pub anywhere on TV – and they take a drink of the disgusting stuff that is in that glass, give them a round of applause, because it's foul.

I would really like to bring out more of my talents; since *Piercing Brightness* I've become a much more active member of the artist creative group and I keep my ear close to the ground. I'm actually seriously considering getting some drama qualifications and going into an acting career.

Stephen Berry

Susan Walsh, *To Scatter*, St. Wilfrid's Church

'Suddenly this music! Sleep retreats like the undertow of a wave in which a child grasps at a half-glimpsed shell, as I do at this cluster of notes, just heard in a dream.'

Andreï Makine – *A Life's Music* (2002)

To Scatter is a short film, made by artist Susan Walsh as a memorial to Irish migrants, particularly those to Preston and the North West. It explores the significance of music and song as a vital way to remember events, people from the past and a way of life left behind. To play music, to sing about important issues, events in the news or to mock or joke about politicians or the wealthy, to sing about traditions, family life, love and tragedy has always been a tool for the poor and disenfranchised to vent their opinions. It is a safe place to keep unwritten views and plot future strategies.

The film features a chandelier made from a set of piano keys. The piano is an instrument, which allows for the integration of Irish music and ballads into an adopted site for meeting and reunion: the church, the public house, the home. This can enable a merging of both Irish and English histories of socialising, worship, contemplation and musical entertainment within a potentially political arena. *To Scatter* was shown over a two-week period in St. Wilfrid's Roman Catholic Church.

April 2010

Nothing to Do with Us
Owen Hatherley

I attended the 'Revisiting Utopia' event on Preston Bus Station in 2012, where the fact that – for once – enthusiasts and councillors were in the same place, meant I got told a very telling nugget of information by a Preston Council member. It was on the subject of a hideous new hotel, next to the equally hideous new buildings of the University of Central Lancashire. He told me that he'd been the only councillor to vote against the hotel in the planning permission process. When asked why, he said 'because it's a terrible piece of architecture'. He was told 'that's nothing to do with us'.

This stuck in my mind when I found that, far from being reprieved, as seemed to be the case for much of 2012, the Bus Station was suddenly given notice of demolition. In a situation in which benefits are being decimated, estates cleared, the NHS privatised and urban planning regulations torn up, it's easy for politicians (and developers) to claim that architecture is a side issue, of interest only to aesthetes (probably southern). So it might seem that the campaign to save Preston's Bus Station from demolition is a distraction from the issue of austerity and what the response to it should be – but, in fact, if there's a better illustration of how austerity works and how hopeless the Labour Party have been in opposing it, I can think of few better examples.

But, first things first – the building itself. Preston Bus Station was designed in the late 1960s by local, later to be

international, architects Building Design Partnership. 'Bus Station' hardly covers what the building is. What we have here is a Bus Station and multi-storey car park, with a vast, airport-lounge-like interior boasting cafes, a newsagent, a hairdresser (!) and so forth – a Public Building in the truest sense; taking a mundane thing and making it as comfortable and pleasing as possible, lack of maintenance notwithstanding. The finishes of the building – the wood, tiles and metal of the interior, the op-art concrete waves of the facade – are of the very highest quality. Nothing today, bar the most expensive 'signature' architecture, is this well-made. But being a good Public Building is not doing a structure many favours today.

When the council voted to demolish, I tried to figure out what was exactly happening with the Bus Station via Twitter, and was still none the wiser. For most of the 2000s the proposal was to demolish the station and replace it – and the surrounding area of the 1960s Markets and office buildings built at the same time by RMJM and BDP – with Tithebarn, a 'mall without walls', inspired by the likes of Liverpool One, or, maybe closer to home, The Rock in Bury – where shopping malls were treated rather dubiously as (privately-owned, privately patrolled) 'streets' rather than enclosed spaces. Always a strange idea in a declining city that already has two large malls, Tithebarn was an early casualty of the recession, effectively cancelled in 2011 when John

Lewis pulled out. That seemed to give the place a reprieve – at 'Revisiting Utopia', local politicians and councillors appeared to be keen to keep the building: the only alleged obstacle was Lancashire County Council, which wanted a new bus station built by the Railway Station. This idea, that it's in 'the wrong place', comes up a lot, although it's puzzling – it's ten minutes' walk from the railway station, but right next to the Guildhall, the Markets, the magnificent Harris Museum & Art Gallery and the shopping centres, basically everything a non-Prestonian might want to see or do in Preston. Nonetheless, Lancs Council are apparently adamant that they will not fund a refurbishment (though it may be cheaper than demolition), so if the current building is demolished, there will (eventually) be a new bus station and LCC will (probably) be funding it. A render was leaked to the public by Preston architect Dominic Roberts – a shockingly nondescript and amateurish piece of PFI design, like replacing the Harris with a Tescos.

Although this is what Lancashire County Council want, they are not planning to do this anytime soon – they are not demanding the Bus Station be cleared out of the way. Why would they, when they want to build it somewhere else entirely? So the reason given is the cost of maintaining the current Bus Station. A recent costing puts this at £23 million, a bizarre figure – earlier estimates put it at £4 million, and even councillors concede the figure is probably around £10 million. Particularly when council budgets are being crushed in Eric Pickles' iron fist, £4 million is a lot of money, but the fact is that the Bus Station costs £300,000 a year to run. Local socialist councillor Michael Lavalette estimates that a 50p increase per parking costs would pay for the building's annual maintenance. So all this suggests that someone, somewhere, wants a prohibitive figure put on the building so that they can make the we-are-protecting-services-not-buildings-for-ponces argument, to get rid of the Bus Station asap. What for, though?

What is key here is that Preston City Council also voted to demolish RMJM's 1960s Market building adjacent. That is, the other council-owned part of the former Tithebarn site. Like the Bus Station, although not quite as architecturally stunning, the Market is a good piece of civic design, and it is well-used. Nonetheless, the Preston City Council meeting that decided to demolish the Bus Station and Markets met for a paltry 30 minutes. I'm sure a lot of people in the city and outside of it have talked more about the Bus Station on an average Monday than that. So it seems pretty obvious that a fix is in. What sort of a fix? Well, what the council want in place of the Bus Station, for the moment, is a surface car park. Given that there's already a cordon sanitaire of dead space between the Bus Station and the ring road, that means a vast, exurban empty space in the middle of the city, to deliberately create the sort of vast, anti-urban car-centred wasteland that has destroyed any hint of urbanity in cities like Southampton – only without the actual shopping mall those spaces serve. The city's idea appears to be – as far as I can tell – that they will carry out the programme of demolition that was meant to precede the Tithebarn scheme, giving them a big empty space that they can then sell to a developer at that mythical moment, *When The Market Picks Up*.

That is, Preston is *choosing* to inflict on itself what Bradford now has, a huge bloody hole where it used to have a city centre. This, incidentally, is also what happened to Portsmouth City Council in 2004, when it demolished the Tricorn Centre, after a similar campaign that pit bluff, don't-know-a-lot-but-I-know-what-I-like councillors against local and national architecture enthusiasts, who proposed several plausible schemes for refurbishment, redesign and renewal to no avail. The Tricorn was replaced with a surface car park, on which a 'Northern Quarter' was meant to be built, when The Market was most definitely Up. Eight years later it hasn't been.

This is the fate that Preston is *choosing* to inflict on itself. If it's only a matter of Lancashire County Council's hostility, why are Preston Council so keen to frame it as being about the Bus Station's allegedly exorbitant expense? Unlike similar acts of philistinism, like Tower Hamlets' sell-offs of Robin Hood Gardens or Henry Moore's 'Old Flo', or Birmingham's flogging off of sites occupied by John Madin's Library and NatWest tower, there are no buyers waiting in the wings. Unlike the Tricorn, the building is structurally sound, it works, and it is popular, winning the *Lancashire Evening Post*'s poll for best building in the city – no mean feat when the Harris is nearby. Like the Tricorn, there are several plausible plans for its redesign and reuse, to sort out its problems with circulation, its excessive size, and so forth. Preston and its architecture have been, through the council's philistinism, in the news for the first time since, well, the 1960s. Every council wants an Iconic, nationally recognised building. Preston now has one. So why not appeal to

Lancashire County Council's good sense, and mount a council-sponsored campaign to save the building? It still seems like the most plausible reason is that they really do *want* to replace the Bus Station with a surface car park, in the hope that one day a developer will want to build them a mall. After (or rather during) the massive game-changer that is the financial crisis and the obvious bankruptcy of cities built on debt, shopping and driving in and out, Labour councillors – in both Lancashire and Preston – still can't think of anything their cities might be other than shopping centres. In fact, austerity now gives them an even better alibi. Can't you see – we've got no choice. *It's nothing to do with us.*

Additional note:
After two unsuccessful attempts, Preston Bus Station was granted Grade II listed building status in September 2013. Since then, plans to demolish the Bus Station have been abandoned. Preston City Council has now given ownership of the building and surroundung land to Lancashire County Council, which has committed £8.5 million to its renovation. This has happened since the last local elections, with Lancashire County Council back to being controlled by the Labour Party. Immediate plans for proper maintenance and/or resoration are as of yet not formulated (April 2014).

The Curatorial Constellation – Durational Public Art, Cohabitational Time and Attentiveness
Paul O'Neill

'As a constellation, theoretical thought circles the concept it would like to unseal, hoping that it will fly open like the lock of a well-guarded safe-deposit box: in response, not to a single key or a single number, but to a combination of numbers.'

Theodor W. Adorno,
Negative Dialectics[1]

In this essay, I will attempt to bridge current discussions around curatorship, public art and urban practice. I will do this by first exploring recent concepts of 'the curatorial' and the ways in which they encompass certain ideas about durationally-specific practice in conjunction with exhibition curating. Secondly, I will briefly draw upon some ideas from a number of longer-term, social and embedded approaches to public art, which have emerged as responses to specific locations in a bid to engage multiple communities – as a critique of the shorter-term, peripatetic projects that have been so prevalent over the past twenty years or so. Thirdly, I will consider the ways in which the idea of 'cohabitational time' is a key attribute within these multifaceted projects, as the means through which the curatorial and durational praxis can be brought closer together. And finally, I will draw upon Alois Riegl's concept of 'attentiveness', as set out in his 1902

essay on Dutch group portraiture, as a way of positing our current condition as post-participatory. In this concept, the borders between the author-producer and the participant-receiver of public art are no longer so clearly attributed. Instead, the end work is produced by fields of interaction between multiple actors and agencies within durationally specific public art praxis.

The Curatorial -as-Constellation

While the open-endedness of recent discussions around the curatorial is undoubtedly somewhat frustrating at times, this very frustration is, perhaps, the objective. Certain articulations of the curatorial have identified a strand of practice that seeks to resist categorical resolution, preferring to function in the Adornian sense, as a constellation of activities that do not wish to fully reveal themselves. Instead of conforming to the logic of inside and outside (in terms of the distribution of labour), a constellation of activities exists in which the exhibition (whichever form it takes) can be one of many component parts. Rather than forcing syntheses, this idea of a constellation (as an always-emergent praxis) brings together incommensurable social objects, ideas and subject relations in order to demonstrate the structural faults and falsities inherent in the notion of the hermetic exhibition as primary curatorial work.

This is evident from the briefest of glances at a number of recent attempts at describing the curatorial. For example, Irit Rogoff articulates the curatorial as critical thought that does not rush to embody itself, instead raising questions that are to be unravelled over time; Maria Lind's notion of the curatorial involves practising forms of political agency that try to go beyond the already known; Beatrice von Bismark's understanding of the curatorial is as a continuous space of negotiation, contributing to other processes of becoming; and Emily Pethick's proposition of the curatorial presupposes an unbounded framework, allowing for things, ideas and outcomes to emerge in the process of being realised.[2] Illustrative of the contested territory around the expanded field of curatorship, these definitions cannot be reduced to a set of positions that exist in opposition to exhibition-making; rather, they support forms of research-based, dialogical practice in which the processual and the serendipitous overlap with speculative actions and open-ended forms of production.

The propositions articulated above consider the curatorial as an interlinked range of concepts, uniting unique forms of practice under a single rubric without pretending to gain exhaustive insight into them. This brings divergent forms of curatorial practice together to self-consciously catalyse each other, while not shying away from the negative, the contradictory or the antithetical.

I would argue that the curatorial – as an open concept – prioritises the many ways and means of working with others, within a temporary space of cooperation, which allows ideas to emerge in the process of doing, speaking and being together. In this sense, the discursive aspect of curatorial work is given parity with – rather than being perceived as contingent upon – the main event of staging gallery-based art exhibitions.

The curatorial, conceived of as a constellation, resists the stasis of the artist-curator-spectator triumvirate and supports more semi-autonomous and self-determined aesthetic and discursive forms of practice that may overlap and intersect, rather than seeking a dialectic (image) or oppositional presentation (form). It is not about being either for or against exhibitions. As a constellation, discursively-led curatorial praxis does not exclude the exhibition as one of its many productive forms. Rather than being either in opposition to one another or integrated, all of these practices propose a more juxtaposed field of signification, form, content and critique. In this sense, the constellation is an ever-shifting and dynamic cluster of changing elements that are always resisting reduction to a single common denominator. By preserving irreconcilable differences, such praxis retains a tension between the universal and the particular, between essentialism and nominalism.

The preservation, or enabling, of these differences is also evident within durational approaches to public art, in which there is a constellation of intersecting ideas and moments of production, with many actors, advisory roles, publics and agencies at work, leading to such a multiplicity of praxis that it makes such projects impossible to grasp in their entirety. Paracuratorial practices are part of this constellation, but they could also be considered types of practice that respond to certain restrictive conditions of production.[3] The work of exhibition-making exists not only to legitimise the paracuratorial work taking place alongside it; rather, processes are set in motion in relation to other actions and events within the curatorial. As such, paracuratorial work attaches itself to, intervenes in, or rubs up against these conditions. Such projects might occur at the points at which the main event is critiqued from within, or when the restrictive scenarios, into which art and curatorial labour are forced, are sidestepped in some way. They employ a host-and-uninvited-guest tactic of coordination and invention, enabling parasitic curatorial labour to exist alongside, or in confrontation with, pre-existing cultural forms, originating scenarios, or prescribed exhibition contexts.

Because of the evasiveness outlined above, there are a number of key issues with discursive, duration-specific practice, such as: what happens to art when its primary objective is not to engage with people and places under nomadic conditions, such as biennial curatorship, but instead gathers its audiences over a longer period than an exhibition-event? What happens when the primary outcome of a durational project is a more dispersed form of mediation, and when the artwork, the authorial voice and the exhibition site are not easy to locate – in other words, when the project does not result in single autonomous works/exhibitions to be viewed as one-off experiences? Does the artwork's objecthood completely disappear into processes of operation, interventionist procedures and 'hard to find' participatory moments? What happens when public participation is

a negotiated space of co-production within multiple networked flows of social encounters? These are just a few of the many questions that processual and cooperative praxis raise.

In light of the above, the cooperative and the processual are difficult to contain or represent. As forms of socially networked projects, they are associated with contextual, durational and dialogical procedures rather than prioritising material outcomes. Looking back over the past twenty years, for example, we find many terms that have been inscribed upon these practices, such as: 'conversational art' (Homi Bhabha), 'dialogical aesthetics' (Grant Kester), 'new genre public art' (Suzanne Lacy), 'new situationism' (Claire Doherty), 'connective aesthetics' (Suzi Gablik), 'participatory art' (Claire Bishop) and 'collective creativity' (WHW). Equally, 'the educational turn' in contemporary art and curating (Paul O'Neill and Mick Wilson) and the emergence of an art of 'social cooperation' (Tom Finkelpearl) have, in different ways, attempted to encapsulate the social and processual qualities inherent in more immaterial forms of both curatorial and artistic co-production, predominantly experienced beyond the art-institutional setting or the traditional gallery frame. To this long list I wish to add the term 'duration-specific' art as a divergent model of practice, in which public *time*, rather than public *space*, is the priority.

Durational Public Art and Cohabitational Time

In order to move beyond the ontological notion of a reflexive subject – in which moving from passive to active participant in art is equally difficult to quantify – contemplation is needed on the issue of time. More specifically on how public time is framed in order that a space of co-production can emerge. This is what Bruno Latour refers to as the need for more 'cohabitational time, the great Complicator', with democratic space being understood as time spent together, publicly, in contradiction with each other. If we are to think of participation as more than a closed, one-off, relational or social interaction with art, it must take account of duration as a temporal process of cohabitation, in which time can contribute to something that is immeasurable, unquantifiable and unknowable from the outset. In this sense, art and its participation can only be experienced durationally, as lived difference.

Durationally-specific praxis accounts for the transitory attribute of time as a means of structuring the fluctuating encounter with art from its attributed place in 'public space' to the production of 'time-places'. In this necessary shift, time is always experienced as hybrid, fluctuating and becoming. The temporality of practice is neither fixed nor clearly bounded to a single location. It is dispersed across time, beyond the duration of the moment when the curator-producer or artist are embedded in place.

Duration is more than the length of time that something continues. It has its own extrinsic values, such as mobility, agency, change or affect.[4] Duration can also involve a process of being together, for a period of time, with some common objectives, often as a means to constitute a new mode of relational, conversational and participatory practice. There tends to be a multiplicity of modes of interaction between people. Duration also has a destabilising effect, because there is no longer a fixed time and place in which to experience, or participate in, the art as event. This is most evident in the fact that a number of people contributing to durational projects are often unaware exactly of what they are taking part in and what the outcome is intended to be; their participation – what has been done, who took part and what was achieved – is not something that can be measured or evaluated in a clear way.

This is not to say that duration as long-termism is the *a priori* solution for progressive public art, but rather that duration aims to problematise the time component of art's engagement with publics. As Dave Beech indicates in his critique of durational-ism, 'Duration is problematic because it is presented as a solution for art's social contradictions, whereas the only viable political solution must be to problematise time for art'.[5] Duration cannot, therefore, become the default that is employed as a solve-all solution. Rather, as will be explored in greater depth in what follows, durationality is characterised by a degree of attentiveness to the outside world, as much as to the dynamics of those individuals involved.

Durationally-specific public art allows for something to emerge over time, as part of its productive process. It is more than a psychological experience – a transitory state of *becoming* – it is also the concrete evolution of creativity, a state of being together within time, which surpasses itself in a manner that makes duration the very material of cooperative creative action. Durationally-specific public art could be seen as embracing more social and cooperative forms of artistic co-production for specific sites, situations or environments, allowing things to unfold over time through various modes of both local and dispersed forms of participation.

This approach is found in a range of practices in which multiple participants are involved as co-creators, such as projects by Tania Bruguera, Pablo Helguera, Jeanne van Heeswijk, Harrell Fletcher, CAMP, Temporary Services, Oda Projesi, Annette Krauss, Skart, Ultra-Red, Hiwa K, Can Altay, MyVillages.org, Park Fiction or certain projects by art and architecture groups such as MUF or Transparadiso. The function of the curatorial proposition is to create situations of potential agency for the co-productive processes initiated by the artist, or curator, as post-autonomous producer. An understanding of the curatorial as an accumulation of interactions is put forward, with the work of art configured as a cluster of interventions gathered together over time, to result in more dispersed forms of distribution. More specifically, durational public art praxis proposes affect as a continuous, open-ended process. This involves taking a holistic, multidimensional approach to designated situations, maximising resources – material, human and economic – using local distinctiveness as a starting point for a vision of the future, engaging professionals to work outside their normal sphere of practice and sharing an awareness of symbolic value. Rather than being overly predetermined, duration-specific projects account for the unplanned as a means of setting things in motion, allowing for ideas to emerge while *doing time* together. In many of these practices, the moment of publicness is never fully revealed. In various ways, these projects show

how the publicness of public art and its curatorship must recognise the significance of engaging audiences and encouraging research-based outcomes that are responsive to their specific contexts, publics and locations over time. Significant in this respect are *The Blue House* (Het Blauwe Huis), IJburg, the Netherlands (2004–2009); *Beyond*, Leidsche Rijn, the Netherlands (1999–2009); *Trekroner Art Plan*, Roskilde, Denmark (2001–present); Grizedale Arts' *Creative Egremont*, Cumbria, UK (ongoing since 1999) and The Serpentine Gallery's *Edgware Road Project*, London, UK (2009–2011). To this list can be added many ongoing projects such as Van Heeswijk's *2 Up 2 Down*, Anfield, Liverpool; *The Food Thing*, initiated by artist Mick Wilson, Dublin; *Slow Prototype*, initiated by curator Nuno Sacramento, at Scottish Sculpture Workshop; *In Certain Places*, Preston (since 2003) and *Our Day Will Come* (2011), a month-long free school project in Hobart, Tasmania.[6] Having already written extensive case studies on some of these projects as part of the publication *Locating the Producers*, there is no need to re-iterate them in depth here.[7] Instead, I will briefly outline Jeanne van Heeswijk's project, *The Blue House*, so as to illustrate the ways in which such non-representational processes of communication and exchange can form the content and structure of the work of art as a kind of paracuratorial practice as outlined above.

The Blue House began with Van Heeswijk sidestepping the original brief of a restrictive site-responsive public art commission, in order to instigate new fields of interaction. Situated in a newly built suburb of Amsterdam called IJburg, she collaborated with the urbanist Dennis Kaspori, and the architect Hervé Paraponaris, in arranging for a large villa in a housing block to be taken off the private market and re-designated as a space for reflection, artistic production and cultural activity. Over a four-year period, from 2005 until 2009, the Blue House Association of the Mind functioned as a changing group of local and international practitioners who took up residence for up to six months each, as part of an open-ended organisational structure. Invitees conducted research, produced works of art, films and publications and were involved in discussions and other activities. This resulted in numerous interventions being made by practitioners in and around *The Blue House*, which responded to the specifics of a place undergoing construction as part of an extensive urban renewal plan. Rather than producing artworks with intrinsic aesthetic values, *The Blue House* was a para-institutional model based on social relationality. The result was the culmination of associated responses to the local context and an organised network of willing participants who collectively contributed to the formation of the house and its related activities. Different levels of participation in the project highlighted the complexities of artistic co-production within the logic of succession, continuity and sustainability in a unitary time and place. The concept of participation in art as an artistic practice was constantly being formed and reformed out of extant social processes and political contestations.

Attentiveness as a Value of Duration

In 1902, the Viennese art historian Alois Riegl applied an understanding of attentiveness to the dynamics of sixteenth-century Dutch group portraiture, which suggested that the individuals represented in, say, a painting by Frans Hals were as attentive to each other as they were to the viewer. For Riegl, a group portrait was 'neither an expanded version of an individual portrait nor, so to speak, a mechanical collection of individual portraits in one picture or representational image: rather it [was] a representation of a free association of autonomous, independent individuals'.[8] According to Riegl, attentiveness inhibited other means of unification between the figures represented in a group portrait, ruling out the possibility that those being portrayed were restricted to a common action or emotion.

Within this concept of attentiveness, Riegl highlighted that there are always two forms of coherence. Firstly, there is an 'internal coherence' between those being portrayed within the artwork, which preserves the qualities of likeness of each depicted subject. Secondly, there is an 'external coherence', which depends upon the individuals within the group being attentive to those around them. Beyond this, Riegl was able to demonstrate that, when internal coherence diminished, it could be compensated for by external coherence being increased. In other words, a group portrait could be made to cohere by implicitly including the spectator – which, for Riegl, was partly achieved through the outward gaze of the figures depicted.

The Curatorial Constellation

In this sense, attentiveness is achieved through an equal consideration of the dynamics of compositional arrangement and the psychological exchanges within the group being portrayed. It is also achieved through narrative devices, established within the picture, which provide links among the individuals within the portrait and between them and the external viewer. The concept of attentiveness may be applied to durational public art, in which the latter can be understood as a type of contemporary group portrait in which equal and simultaneous 'attention' is given by participants to each other, and to their immediate environment. Internal cohesion is achieved through mutual attentiveness between the protagonists within the group, and external coherence is encouraged in relation to their surroundings and the world outside the group. In this way, reciprocity may be created, through inter-relationships that are both internal and external to the group of participants, players, actors, performers, actions and spectators.

In progressive duration-specific public art, the necessity of a practice of attentiveness proposes a multiplicity of identities that shift around while questioning how to contribute towards curatorial work as multiple self-image and socialised group portrait. Practitioners must simultaneously become hosts to and guests of each other, as much as playing their part within a semi-autonomous cooperative curatorial labour. Frames of social and human interaction are put in place, to enable the discursive and material production of art. The result can be a cumulative process of semi- public cooperation, whereby ideas of publicness, hospitality and citizenship offer both imaginative and tangible potential.

This essay was developed from a lecture delivered at the conference 'Planning Unplanned – Exploring the New Role of the Urban Practitioner', 19–20 November, 2012. It was co-commissioned by ReaKt, Guimaraes, 2012, Portugal.

1.   Theodor W. Adorno, *Negative Dialectics* Continuum, 2007, p.163.

2.   See Irit Rogoff, 'Smuggling – A Curatorial Model' in Vanessa Joan Müller and Nicolaus Schafhausen, eds., *Under Construction: Perspectives on Institutional Practice*, Walther König, 2006, pp. 132–33; Maria Lind, 'The Curatorial', *Artforum*, October, 2009, pp.103–05; Beatrice von Bismarck, 'Curatorial Criticality: On the Role of Freelance Curators in the Field of Contemporary Art', in Marianne Eigenheer, ed., *Curating Critique*, Revolver, 2007, pp.62–69; and Emily Pethick, 'The Dog that Barked at the Elephant in the Room', *The Exhibitionist*, issue 4, pp.81–82.

3.   *The Exhibitionist* formalised the term 'paracuratorial' in issue 4 (June 2011) and invited three writers – Vanessa Joan Müller, Lívia Páldi and Emily Pethick – to elaborate on its implications for curatorial practice. See also Paul O'Neill, 'The Curatorial Constellation and the Paracuratorial Paradox', *The Exhibitionist*, issue 6, June 2012, pp.55–60.

4.   For an introductory analysis on Bergsonisms, see Suzanne Guerlac, *Thinking in Time: An Introduction to Henri Bergson*, Cornell University, 2006, pp.1–13.

5.   See Dave Beech 'The ideology of

Duration in the Dematerialised Monument', in Paul O'Neill and Claire Doherty, eds., *Locating the Producers: Durational Approaches to Public Art*, Valiz, 2011, pp.313–26.

6.   *Our Day Will Come*, co-curated by Fiona Lee and Paul O'Neill, was a month-long durational project. Housed in the central courtyard of the University of Tasmania, School of Art in Hobart, the project used a pedagogical framework not so much to educate, through a democratic substitute, but to facilitate a platform for generative discourse. This mode of production was entirely contingent upon the collaboration of others. Participants would sign up for the 'school within a school', which was physically located in a small 1950s portable council tea hut, strategically positioned in the courtyard at the entrance of the institution. Rather than being antagonistic, the odd relationship between the two schools created a symbiotic affiliation in which the big school fed off the little school and vice versa. A four-week iterative structure lent itself to the idea of a syllabus or curriculum which was delivered around the asking of its participant body a key questions each week: What is a school? What is usefulness? What is autonomy? What is remoteness? The concept of Socratic dialogue – based upon the asking and answering of questions – was a tactical move that aimed to drive cooperative production, which included a series of school workshops, plays, a radio station, performances, events, four dinners, a disco and a conference in a nightclub. The project involved bringing together a core group of invested participants, to work alongside nine international artists: Mick Wilson, Rhona Byrne, Annie Fletcher and Jem Noble, who came to Hobart, with Sarah Pierce, Garrett Phelan, Gareth Long, Liam Gillick and David Blamey delivering works remotely. The artists produced dialogical, performative and social works of art that did not so much seek to answer O'Neill's questions as to set up the possibility for further engagement and discourse with the collaborating participants. Additionally, artists, writers and theorists from across the world gave further input remotely, which was disseminated through the production of a weekly 'zine that captured the dialogue around the week's question. The project took place in the context of 'Iteration: Again', curated by David Cross. See http://www.iterationagain.com.

7.   See O'Neill and Doherty, eds., op. cit., 2011.

8.   Alois Riegl, cited in Margaret Iverson's *Alois Riegl: Art History and Theory*, The MIT Press, 1993, p.100.

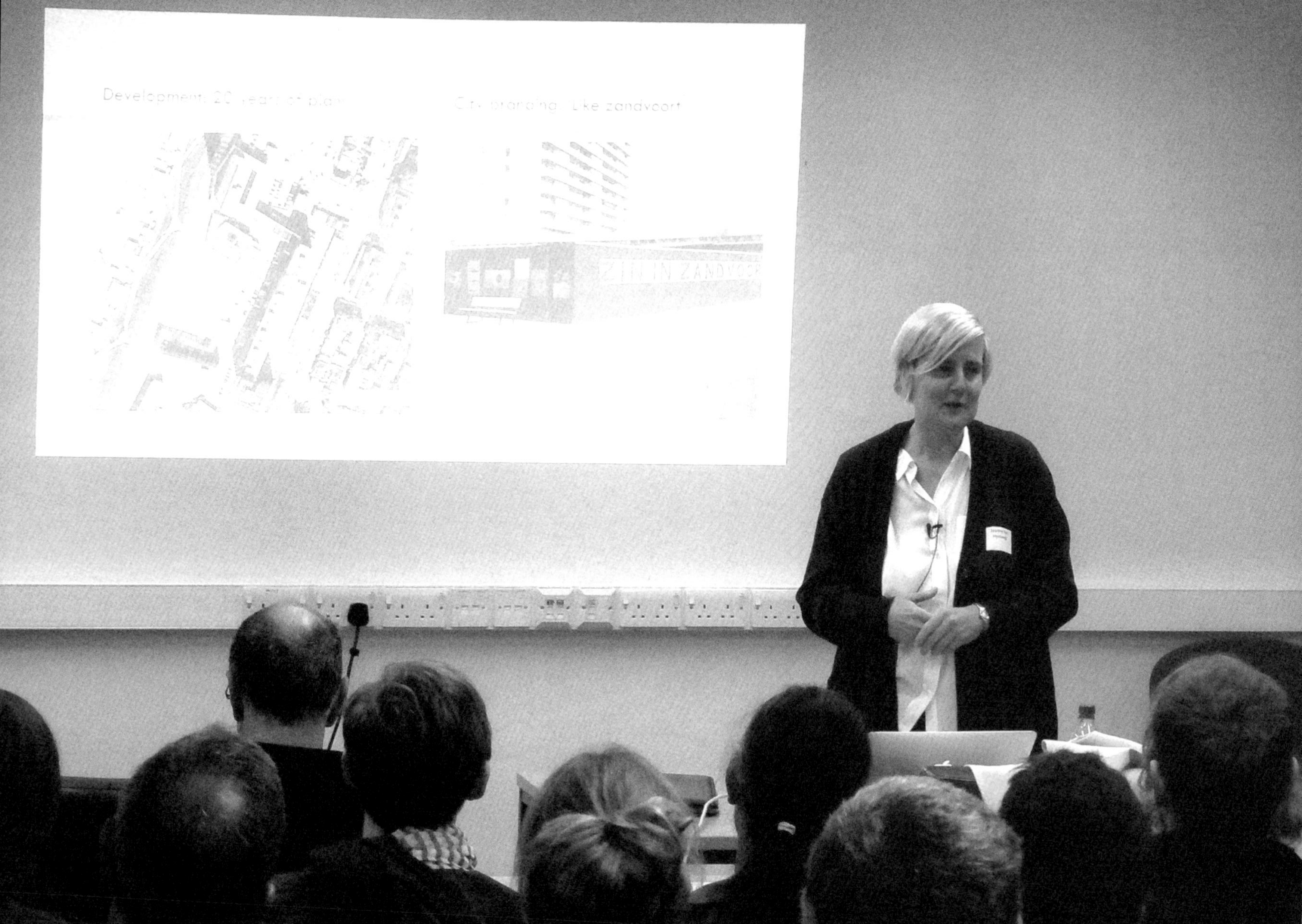
Like zandvoort

Subplots to a City

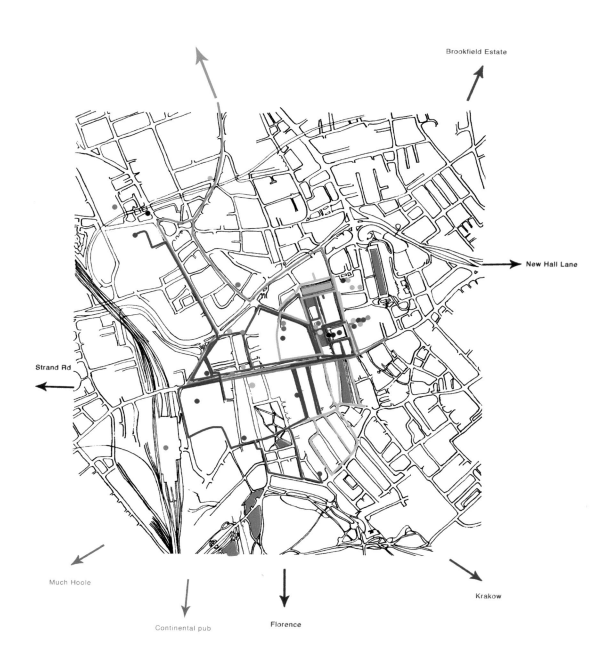

Brookfield Estate

New Hall Lane

Strand Rd

Much Hoole

Continental pub

Florence

Krakow

Amplifying Civic Space

■ Harris Flights   ▨ Charlie MacKeith - The Monument and the Changing City Symposium

▨ Jeppe Hein - Appearing Rooms   ■ Laurence Payot and Jenny Steele - Preston Remembers

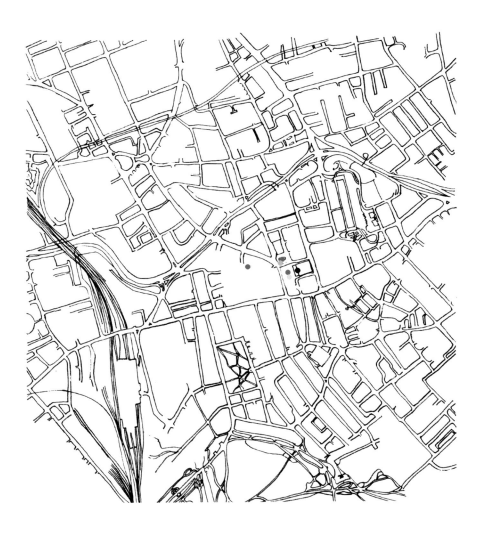

The City and the Changing Economy

Open City Preston 2013

Teresa and Dominique Hodgson-Holt, Martin Hamblen, Leo Fitzmaurice - In The Shops Now!

Catriona Stamp - Banks and Buskers: Contrasting threads making the fabric of Fishergate

Becky Shaw - Local Colour

Katja van Driel and Wouter Osterholt - Open to the Public

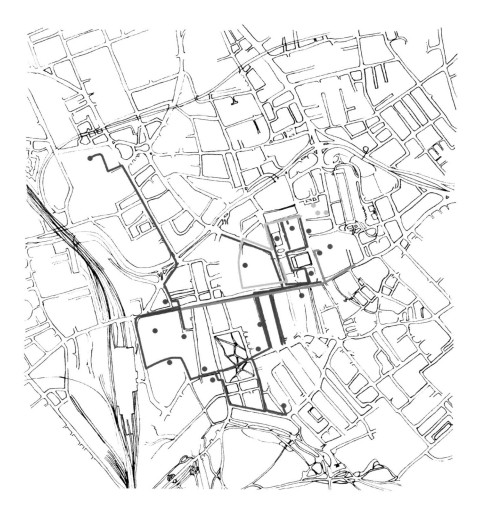

Senses of a City

■ Lisa Wigham - The Waiting Room   ■ Chantal Oakes - Thoughts that Make Actions in the World

■ David Henckel - The Transit of Venus   ■ John Newling - The Preston Market Mystery Project

■ Patricia Walsh - Remote Viewing

Arkwrights Brewery

Much Hoole

Continental pub

Place beyond Place

■ Magda Stawarska-Beavan - The Arcade

□ Place Beyond Place Symposium

■ Shezad Dawood - Piercing Brightness

■ Iain Broadley - The Black Parade

■ Collaborative Space - The Gates of Paradise

□ Susan Walsh - To Scatter

■ Blast Theory - Can You See Me Now?

■ Chris Davis - The Family Project

■ Pam Holmes - Beside the Seaside...

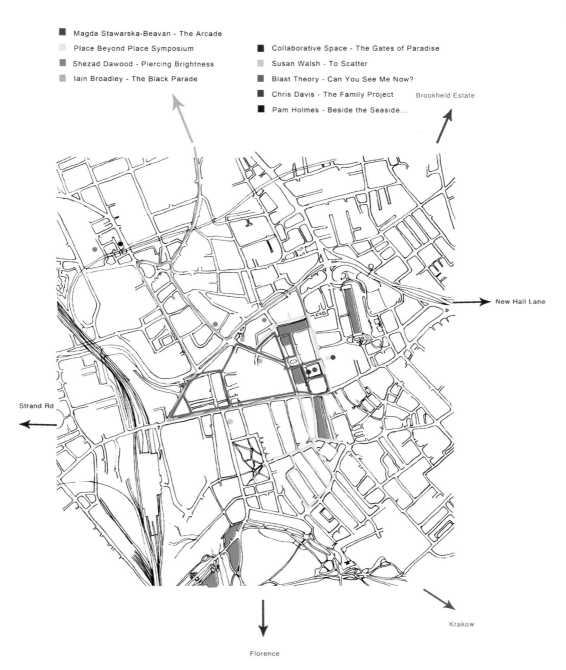

Brookfield Estate

New Hall Lane

Strand Rd

Krakow

Florence

Collaboration Constellations

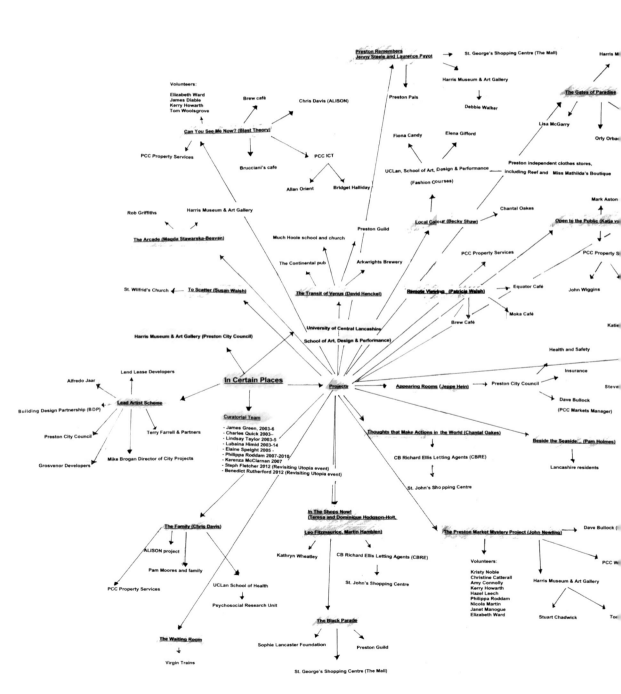

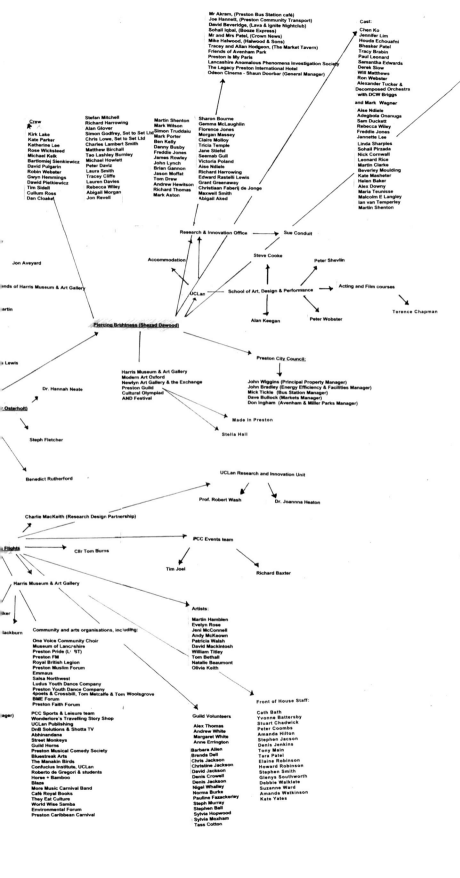

Mr Akram, (Preston Bus Station café)
Joe Hannett, (Preston Community Transport)
David Beveridge, (Lava & Ignite Nightclub)
Sohail Iqbal, (Booze Express)
Mr and Mrs Patel, (Crown News)
Mike Halwood, (Halwood & Sons)
Tracey and Allan Hodgeon, (The Market Tavern)
Friends of Avenham Park
Preston is My Paris
Lancashire Anomalous Phenomena Investigation Society
The Legacy Preston International Hotel
Odeon Cinema - Shaun Doorbar (General Manager)

Cast:
Chen Ko
Jennifer Lim
Houda Echouafni
Bhasker Patel
Tracy Brabin
Paul Leonard
Samantha Edwards
Derek Siow
Will Matthews
Ron Webster
Alexander Tucker & Decomposed Orchestra with DCW Briggs
and Mark Wagner
Aise Ndiele
Adegbola Onanuga
Sam Duckett
Rebecca Wiley
Freddie Jones
Jannette Lee
Linda Sharples
Sohail Pirzada
Nick Cornwall
Leonard Rice
Martin Clarke
Beverley Moulding
Kate Masheter
Helen Baker
Alex Downy
Maria Teunisse
Malcolm E Langley
Ian van Temperley
Martin Shenton

Extras
Alex Greenwood
Kelly Bridge
Malcolm Langley
Liz Henfield
Ria Teunisse
Ross Hewitt
Bradley Clarke
Paul Stewart
Heather Stewart
Mike Coombes
Janis Zelinis
Sultan Hussain
Imogen Walker
Sophie Bracegirdle
Heather Schulz
Hannah-Kate Dickinson
Carrie Thacker
Ruth Scott
Amy Easthem
Nick Cornwall
Stephen Harris
Anita Gallagher
Stephen Mullen
Grace Osbourne
khalia khan
Marsha Hall
Steph Fletcher
Angela
Ben
Aneta
Dawn Ellison
Sarah Armstrong
Liam Best
John Critchley
Lindsay Taylor
Robert Halsall
Helen Hounsell
Paul Hilton
Daniel Iddon
Stephen Ireland
Soyab Khan
Stuart Longshaw
Joe Mansfield
John Mansfield
Thomas Margarson
Scott Mead
Akeel Mirza
Zeshan Pirzada
Gavin Rae
Amy Ramsden
Emma Robinson
Andrea Ronan Clarke
Jane Sharples
Ryan Staveley
Tima Totana
Jasmin Toussaint
Shane Welsh
Matilda Hadcock
Sophie L Cox
B. R. Clarke
Danny Doherty
Camilla Hadcock
Kate Hawarth
Patricia Ovin
Ben Rutherford
Aidan Smart
Liam Taylor
Natasha Allen
Gillian I Bennett
Charlotte Calland
Jodie Cartwright
DJ Clapham
Jack Coole
Claire Corrin
Ethan Couill
David Evans
Dorothy Evans
Paul Gunson
Mike Gregory
Ben Grimn
Kane Halsall
Michelle Halsall

Dorothy Evans
Rebecca Wiley
Paul Humphreys
Louise Sharples
Aiden Smart
Rita Sharples
Peter Wareing
Rosemary McLean
Hollie Mclean
Stephen Berry
Patricia Guerra
Haddis Mostofi
Sam Broadley

Crew
Kirk Lake
Kate Parker
Katherine Lee
Rose Wicksteed
Michael Keik
Bartlomiej Sienkiewicz
David Pulgarin
Robin Webster
Gwyn Hemmings
Dawid Pietkiewicz
Tim Sidell
Cullum Ross
Dan Cloake

Stefan Mitchell
Richard Harrowing
Alan Glover
Simon Godfrey, Set to Set Ltd
Chris Lowe, Set to Set Ltd
Charles Lambert Smith
Matthew Birchall
Tao Lashley Burnley
Michael Howlett
Peter Daviz
Laura Smith
Tracey Cliffe
Lauren Davies
Rebecca Wiley
Abigail Morgan
Jon Revell

Martin Shenton
Mark Wilson
Simon Truddaiu
Mark Porter
Ben Kelly
Danny Busby
Freddie Jones
James Rowley
John Lynch
Brian Gannon
Jason Moffat
Tom Drew
Andrew Hewitson
Richard Thomas
Mark Aston

Sharon Bourne
Gemma McLaughlin
Florence Jones
Morgan Massey
Claire Molloy
Tricia Temple
Jane Stiefel
Seemab Gull
Victoria Poland
Aise Ndiele
Richard Harrowing
Edward Rastelli Lewis
Grant Greenaway
Christiaan Faberij de Jonge
Maxwell Smith
Abigail Aked

Jon Aveyard

iends of Harris Museum & Art Gallery

artin

Research & Innovation Office — Sue Conduit

Accommodation

Steve Cooke

Peter Shevlin

Acting and Film courses

UCLan — School of Art, Design & Performance

Alan Keegan — Peter Wobster

Terence Chapman

Piercing Brightness (Shezad Dawood)

Osterholt)

Steph Fletcher

Benedict Rutherford

a Lewis

Dr. Hannah Neate

Harris Museum & Art Gallery
Modern Art Oxford
Newlyn Art Gallery & the Exchange
Preston Guild
Cultural Olympiad
AND Festival

Preston City Council:
John Wiggins (Principal Property Manager)
John Bradley (Energy Efficiency & Facilities Manager)
Mick Tickle (Bus Station Manager)
Dave Bullock (Markets Manager)
Don Ingham (Avenham & Miller Parks Manager)

Made In Preston

Stella Hall

UCLan Research and Innovation Unit

Prof. Robert Wash

Dr. Joannna Heaton

Charlie MacKeith (Research Design Partnership)

Flights

PCC Events team

Cllr Tom Burns

Tim Joel

Richard Baxter

Harris Museum & Art Gallery

iker

lackburn

Community and arts organisations, including:
One Voice Community Choir
Museum of Lancashire
Preston Pride (LGBT)
Preston FM
Royal British Legion
Preston Muslim Forum
Emmaus
Salsa Northwest
Ludus Youth Dance Company
Preston Youth Dance Company
4poets & Crossbill, Tom Metcalfe & Tom Woolsgrove
BME Forum
Preston Faith Forum

ager)

PCC Sports & Leisure team
Wonderlore's Travelling Story Shop
UCLan Publishing
DnB Solutions & Shotta TV
Abhinandana
Street Monkeys
Guild Horns
Preston Musical Comedy Society
Bluestreak Arts
The Manakin Birds
Confucius Institute, UCLan
Roberto de Gregori & students
Horse + Bamboo
Blaze
More Music Carnival Band
Café Royal Books
They Eat Culture
World Wise Samba
Environmental Forum
Preston Caribbean Carnival

Artists:
Martin Hamblen
Evelyn Rose
Jeni McConnell
Andy McKeown
Patricia Walsh
David Mackintosh
William Titley
Tom Bethall
Natalie Beaumont
Olivia Keith

Front of House Staff:
Cath Bath
Yvonne Battersby
Stuart Chadwick
Peter Coombs
Amanda Hilton
Stephen Jacson
Denis Jenkins
Tony Main
Tara Patel
Elaine Robinson
Howard Robinson
Stephen Smith
Glenys Southworth
Debbie Walklate
Suzanne Ward
Amanda Watkinson
Kate Yates

Guild Volunteers
Alex Thomas
Andrew White
Margaret White
Anne Errington
Barbara Allen
Brenda Dell
Chris Jackson
Christine Jackson
David Jackson
Denis Crowell
Denis Jackson
Nigel Whalley
Norma Burke
Pauline Fazackerley
Steph Murray
Stephen Ball
Sylvia Hopwood
Sylvia Moxham
Tass Cotton

Archive

Date	In Certain Places	Preston	Regional/ National/ International
1989		James Green begins working at the Harris Musem & Art Gallery	Richard Serra's *Tilted Arc* is removed from Federal Plaza in New York
			start of work on 'Public Art Strategy for Cardiff Bay', the first such strategy in the UK (published 1991)
1990		Charles Quick begins working at Lancashire Polytechnic	'Public Art Report' published by the Public Art Forum
			'Edge90' takes place in Newcastle, London, and Glasgow
1991			Art for Architecture scheme established by the RSA (closed in 2004)
1992		Preston Guild, includes temporary sculpture project devised by Val Murray and Charles Quick with second-year sculpture students from Lancashire Polytechnic	Documenta X, Kassel
			Commissions East established in Cambridge
			M8 Art Project – with commissions along the motorway between Glasgow and Edinburgh – starts
			Susan Lacy coins term 'new genre public art'
1993		Lancashire Polytechnic becomes the University of Central Lancashire	Rachel Whiteread's *House* installed in East London (demolished January 1994)
		'Do You?', a one-day event in the Flag Market, which involved UCLan sulpture students working with prisoners at Garth Prison, and the Harris Museum & Art Gallery's Education Officer, Bob Martin	Locus+ established in Newcastle
1994			National Lottery is established
1997			second Munster Sculpture Project
			Documenta XI, Kassel
			Guggenheim Museum opens in Bilbao
			Labour wins the UK national elections
1998		Grosvenor Ltd. and Preston Council begin working on the Tithebarn scheme	Anthony Gormley's *Angel of the North* unveiled
		'The Harris Museum Project' (curated with Stuart Wilson) begins	'arttranspennine98' organised by Tate Liverpool and Henry Moore Foundation, Leeds
			Richard Rogers appointed Chair of the Urban Task Force, set up by the government to 'identify the causes of urban decline in England and recommend practical solutions to bring people back into our cities, towns and urban neighbourhoods' (UTF, 1999)

Timeline

Date	In Certain Places	Preston	Regional/ National/ International
1999		*Puddle* by Keith Wilson (called off last-minute by Preston Council Health & Safety officer)	North West Development agency launched by New Labour
			Commission for Architecture and the Built Environment (CABE) established
			Mark Wallinger's *Ecce Homo* is installed on Fourth Plinth in Trafalgar Square, London
			Liverpool Biennial established
			Janet Cardiff's *The Missing Voice (case study b)* launched
2000		*Interruptions* project at the Harris Museum & Art Gallery and St. Peter's church, UCLan by Charles Quick	Public Art Online – a major resource on art in the public realm – is launched by Public Art South West
			Platform for Art is established at London Underground
			Public Art Network established by Americans for the Arts
2001		National Football Museum opens in Deepdale, Preston	Modus Operandi develops public art programme for new BBC's Broadcasting House redevelopment (realised in 2004)
			Jeremy Deller's *The Battle of Orgreave* enacted
2002		Preston awarded city status	Documenta XI, Kassel
			Liverpool Biennial
			Situations established in Bristol
2003	In Certain Places formed	Tithebarn Scheme announced	'artstranspennine03'
	Alfredo Jaar visits Preston for the first time, gives presentation at UCLan and runs 'visioning session' at Townhall for Grosvenor and city stakeholders	Simon Starling, *East Doors (North)* at Harris Museum & Art Gallery	
2004	Terry Farrell lecture at UCLan and exhibition at the Harris Museum & Art Gallery		'Culture at the Heart of Regeneration' published by the Department for Culture Media and Sport
	Lubaina Himid begins curating 'Talking on Corners' programme		ixia (formerly Public Art Forum) is established in Birmingham, as a think tank and research organisation for public art, funded by Arts Council
	'Speaking of Art' programme, curated by Ian Banks, begins (November 2004–July 2005)		
	Charles Quick and Alfredo Jaar appointed as Lead Artists for the Tithebarn scheme (December)		Liverpool Biennial
2005	Elaine Speight begins working for In Certain Places	City Brand project set up at UCLan, led by Prof. Ben Casey	Marc Quinn's *Alison Lapper Pregnant* installed on Fourth Plinth in Trafalgar Square, London
	'Speaking of Art – Urban View' programme, with David Hunt, Iain Borden and Andreas Lang	completion of development agreement between Grosvenor and Preston City Council	Anish Kapoor's *Cloud Gate* installed at Millennium Park, Chicago
			Christo & Jeanne-Claude's *Gates* installed in Central Park, New York

Archive

Date	In Certain Places	Preston	Regional/ National/ International
2006	'Speaking of Art – Future City' programme, with John Newling, Melissa Mean, Mike Brogan, John Joughin, Laurie Peake and Becky Shaw Jeppe Hein, *Appearing Rooms*; Pam Holmes, *Beside the Seaside...*; Patricia Walsh, *Remote Viewing* (July)	'Arts Council Art 06' event takes place in Preston (June) PAD Gallery opens in Church Street	Liverpool Biennial
2007	John Newling, *The Preston Market Mystery Project* (November 2007–June 2008) Kerenza McClarnan appointed as Project Manager for 7 months Charles Quick and Alfredo Jaar make public presentation (March) Chris Davis, *The Family* begins (ends May 2008) Blast Theory, *Can You See Me Now?* (July)	'Prestival' (July) John Lewis announce plans to be the anchor store in Tithebarn development Grosvenor Ltd. & Lend Lease form partnership (March) Preston Tithebarn LTD partnership legally formalised (July)	third Munster Sculpture Project Documenta 12, Kassel
2008	Chantal Oakes, *Thoughts That Make Actions in the World* (February) Philippa Roddam appointed as Project Assistant for 2.5 years Becky Shaw, *Local Colour* (July-November) Charles Quick and Alfredo Jaar talk at BDP in London (March)	PAD moves to the Post Office Planning application for Tithebarn submitted (September)	world economy crashes Liverpool European City for Culture Liverpool Biennial Liverpool One opens (May) first Folkestone Triennial
2009	'In the Shops Now!', with Leo Fitzmaurice, Martin Hamblen, Teresa and Dominique Hodgson-Holt (July–August)	Grovenor pull out of Tithebarn scheme (October)	
2010	Magda Stawarska-Beavan, *The Arcade* (April) Susan Walsh, *To Scatter* (April) 'Place beyond Place' symposium, with Loraine Leeson, Paul Goodwin, Rebecca Chesney, Catriona Stamp, William Titley	PAD Closes Tithebarn public enquiry begins (May)	Conservative Party and Liberal Democrats form coalition after UK national elections CABE abolished and merged with the Design Council to become Design Council CABE Liverpool Biennial
2011	'The Monument and the Changing City' symposium, with presentations by Charlie MacKeith, Lubaina Himid, Chris Meigh-Andrews, Paul Gough, Alan Rice, Jonathan Vickery Shezad Dawood, filming of *Piercing Brightness* & public talk special edit of *Piercing Brightness* shown at FACT for AND festival, with live soundtrack by Acid Mothers Temple *Piercing Brightness* exhibition at the Harris Museum & Art Gallery	BBC Passion Play staged at Preston Bus Station (Easter) drive-in cinema in Covered Markets, developed by AND Festival and They Eat Culture, supported by In Certain Places (September) John Lewis withdraws from Tithbarn (November) Tithebarn scheme abandoned Preston City Council gains a Labour majority	second Folkestone Triennial

Timeline

Date	In Certain Places	Preston	Regional/ National/ International
2012	'Revisiting Utopia' symposium, with presentations by Owen Hatherley and Irena Bauman, and contributions by Cllr. Tom Burns, Cllr. Keven Ellard and Christina Malathouni	Preston Guild The National Football Museum moves to Manchester	North West Development Agency abolished (March) Documenta 13, Kassel Liverpool Biennial
	Bus Station exhibition in the old Post Office, curated by Steph Fletcher and Benedict Rutherford		
	Piercing Brightness exhibition at Modern Art Oxford (spring)		
	Piercing Brightness exhibition at Newlyn Art Gallery and The Exchange (summer)		
	'Preston Remembers' with artwork by Jenny Steele and Laurence Payot		
	Piercing Brightness receives Jarman runner up award, and is screened at the Whitechapel Art Gallery, London		
	'Subplots to a City', with artworks by David Henckel, Jeni McConnel and Hannah Elizabeth Allan, Lisa Wigham, Iain Broadley		
	Preston premiere of *Piercing Brightness* at the Odeon cinema		
2013	Katja van Driel and Wouter Osterholt, *Open to the Public* (January)	work begins on Cenotaph redevelopment (May) work should have begun on original Tithebarn plan (summer) Preston Bus Station given Grade II heritage listed status (September) Preston awarded City Deal funding Preston Bus Station Parade (November)	
	Charlie MacKeith and Charles Quick, *Harris Flights* (September)		
	'Open City' symposium, with presentations by John Thorp, Paul Swinney, Jess Southern, Jeanne van Heeswijk, and workshops run by Ann Vanner, Hannah Neate, Gisele Bone, Charles Quick		
	Piercing Brightness screened at the ICA, London and touring to art house cinemas across the UK		
	In Certain Places moves to UCLan		
	Piercing Brightness shown at Kino Kino in Norway		
	Piercing Brightness trailer shown in Art in General in New York		
	edit of *Piercing Brightness* shown on C4 Random Acts (March)		
2014		Preston Bus Station handed over to Lancashire County Council	Liverpool Biennial third Folkestone Triennial
2018		Tithebarn scheme scheduled completion (spring)	

Contributors' Biographies

OWEN HATHERLEY is a writer and journalist based in London who writes primarily on architecture, politics and culture. His first book *Militant Modernism* (Zero Books) was published in 2009. His book *A Guide to the New Ruins of Great Britain* (Verso) was published in 2010. Hatherley has also written for a wide range of magazines and newspapers, including *Building Design*, *The Guardian*, *Icon*, the *London Review of Books*, *New Humanist*, the *New Statesman*, *Socialist Review* and *Socialist Worker*. He sits on the editorial boards of *Archinect* and *Historical Materialism*, and has maintained three blogs: *Sit down man, you're a bloody tragedy*, *The Measures Taken* and *Kino Fist*.

LUBAINA HIMID MBE is Professor of Contemporary Art at the University of Central Lancashire. Over the past 30 years she has participated in exhibitions, publications and conferences in the UK and internationally, most recently co-curating 'Thin Black Line(s)' at Tate Britain (2012). Solo shows include Peg Alston in New York (2008), St. Jorgens Museum in Bergen (2001), Tate St. Ives (1999), Transmission in Glasgow (1994), and Chisenhale Gallery in London (1989). She represented Britain at the 5th Havana Biennale (1994) and has shown work at the Studio Museum in New York (1997), Track 17 in Los Angeles (1997), the Fine Art Academy in Vienna and the Grazer Kunstverein (both 1990). Her work can be found in a wide range of public collections including Tate, the Victoria & Albert Museum, Arts Council England, Manchester Art Gallery, and the Harris Museum & Art Gallery in Preston.

SOPHIE HOPE is an artist, curator and lecturer. She tries to inspect the uncertain relationships between art and society, which involves establishing how to declare her politics through her practice, rethinking what it means to be paid to be critical and devising tactics to challenge notions of authorship. Since co-founding the curatorial partnership B+B in 2000, she has gone on to pursue her independent practice with projects such as *Critical Friends* (2008–ongoing), a participant-led investigation into socially engaged art; *The Wild Spirits of Efford* (2010), her first radio play; and *Het Reservaat* (2007) a large-scale community performance in a Dutch new town. Her writing and workshops deal with issues of public art, the politics of socially engaged art and curating as critical practice. She is a lecturer on the MA in Arts Policy and Management, Birkbeck, University of London.

PAUL O'NEILL is a curator, writer and educator. He has co-curated over 50 exhibition projects internationally. Since 2013 he is Director Graduate Program at CCS Bard. Until recently, he directed the major international research programme 'Locating the Producers' at Situations, Bristol. Paul's writing has been published widely. He is editor of the curatorial anthology *Curating Subjects* (2007), and co-editor of *Curating and the Educational Turn* with Mick Wilson (2010), both published by de Appel and Open Editions. He is author of *Locating the Producers: Durational Approaches to Public Art* (Valiz, 2011) and *The Culture of Curating, the Curating of Culture(s)*, (The MIT Press, 2012). He is co-editor of *Curating Research* (Open Edition/ de Appel, 2014).

BECKY SHAW is an artist whose work focuses on the relationship between people and the material world. Her artworks respond to places where people and objects interact – in large social environments, including hospitals and factories. Many have involved collaborations with diverse people, ranging from engineers, to performers, hospital residents and scientists, and her PhD research explored making sculpture with palliative care patients. Her work has been included in books such as *From Studio to Situation* (Black Dog, 2004), *The Community Performance Reader* (Routledge, 2007), and *Speculative Strategies* (Underwing Press, 2014). In 2000–2006, she was co-director of Static, an experimental art and architecture gallery in Liverpool. She is Course Leader in Creative Practice at Sheffield Hallam University.

ELAINE SPEIGHT is a research associate at the University of Central Lancashire, where she curates the In Certain Places programme. Her research interests include the capacity of art to interrogate, mediate and disrupt the connections between people and place, and the relationship between art practice and research. As a curator, artist and educator, Elaine has worked for organisations including Liverpool Biennial, Up Projects, Creative Partnerships and Birkbeck, University of London. She has also initiated a number of independent collaborative projects, such as 'Pest' – a series of publications and commissions, which explore artist-led initiatives in the UK, Europe and Canada.

JONATHAN VICKERY is Associate Professor and MA Programme Director in the Centre for Cultural Policy Studies, University of Warwick, and founding Director of the MA Arts, Enterprise and Development. He has been a Henry Moore research fellow, Director of The Aesthesis Project, and executive editorial board member of *Aesthesis: International Journal of Art and Aesthetics in Management and Organizational Life*, and reviews editor and regular contributor to *Art & Architecture Journal*. He has published articles on public art, regeneration and art theory and also worked as an art critic. His area of research is concerned with cultural politics and the public sphere. He has worked with artists creating intellectual dialogue and his own understanding of the conditions of contemporary art.

CHARLES QUICK is the co-founder and Director of In Certain Places. Charles has nearly 40 years experience in contemporary art in public places, as both practitioner and curator. He is a Professor of Public Art Practice at the University of Central Lancashire, where he co-founded the MA in Site and Archive Intervention. Since 2006 he has completed three large-scale commissions along the northeast coast of England, the most notable being *Flash@Hebburn*. The Art and Architecture Journal Press has published a book on the project, *Flash@Hebburn. Urban Art in the New Century*. His work is held in the collections of Wakefield City Art Gallery, Leeds City Art Gallery, and the Henry Moore Institute. His career is recorded through the British Library sound archive Artists' Lives project. He has received awards from HEFCE, Arts Council England, and the British Council.

Image Credits